The Æneid of Virgil

THE ÆNEID OF VIRGIL

VIRGIL

BOOKS I-VI

TRANSLATED BY

HARLAN HOGE BALLARD

BOSTON AND NEW YORK
HOUGHTON, MIFFLIN AND COMPANY
The Riverside Press, Cambridge
1902

K

THIS BOOK

IS

AFFECTIONATELY DEDICATED

To my Father

THE ÆNEID

BOOK I

War is my song, and the man, who first from the
    Ilian seashore,
Banished by fate, into Italy came, and Lavinian
    harbors ;
Long was he driven o'er land and sea by the fury
    of Heaven,
Through the vindictive wrath of implacable Juno ;
    afflicted
Cruelly also by war, or ever he founded a city,   5
Bearing his gods into Latium, whence the proud
    race of the Latins,
Sires of the Alban town, and the city of Rome in
    her glory.
    Tell me the reasons, O Muse, in what was her
    sovereignty wounded,
Or, embittered by what did the queen of the gods
    doom a hero
Signal in faith to endure so many reverses of for-
    tune,
So many burdens to bear ? Are such the resent-   10
    ments of Heaven ?
    There was a city of lu, by Tyrian colonists
    peopled,

Carthage, opposite Rome, and the far distant
    mouths of the Tiber,
Rich in treasures of gold, and of desperate daring
    in battle.
This one Juno is said to have loved above all other
    countries,   15
Samos, herself, less dear; and here were her arms
    and her war-car.
Nay, even then, had the goddess both hope and in-
    tention of making
Carthage queen of the world, — if only the Fates
    would permit it.
But she had heard that a people of Teucrian blood
    was arising,
Destined in future years to level her Tyrian cas-
    tles;   20
Hence was a nation to come, wide ruling, and
    mighty in battle,
So had the Fates decreed, to Libya's utter destruc-
    tion.
Fearful of this, and remembering also the earlier
    conflict
Which she had formerly waged at Troy for her
    well-beloved Argos, —
Nor even yet had her reasons for wrath and her
    bitter repinings   25
Faded away from her mind; still rankled the judg-
    ment of Paris
Deep in her wounded heart, and the scornful con-
    tempt of her beauty,
Also the rival race, and Ganymede's high exalta-
    tion; —
Therefore incensed, was Saturnia driving the
    storm-beaten Trojans,

All that were left by the Greeks and spared by
    cruel Achilles,   30
Far from the Latian shore, and, thus by the Fates
    hurried onward,
Sea after sea did they roam, and year after year
    did they wander ;
Such was the infinite toil of founding the race of
    the Romans.
    Scarcely out of sight of Sicilian land they were
      gladly
Spreading their sails for the deep, and with brazen
    keel plowing the sea-foam,   35
When, the undying wound in her bosom still cher-
    ishing, Juno
Thus with herself communed : " Am I to abandon
    the struggle ·
Vanquished, and Italy yield to the king of the
    Teucrian people ?
I am o'erruled, forsooth, by the Fates ! Was Pal-
    las, then, able
Vessels of Argos to burn, and the sailors to sink
    in the ocean,   40
All for the crime and the madness of one, Oïlean
    Ajax ?
She the consuming fire of Jupiter hurled from the
    storm-cloud,
Scattered their foundering ships, and upturned the
    sea with a tempest.
Him, out-breathing flame from his breast trans-
    pierced by the lightning,
High on a splintering rock she impaled with the
    rush of the whirlwind.   45
I, notwithstanding, who move as Queen of the
    gods, and the sister,

Nay, as the consort of Jove, for so many years,
    with one nation,
Carry on war. And henceforth will any one re-
    verence Juno's
Will, or with bended knee lay a suppliant's gift
    on her altar?"
Silently pondering thus in her wrath-kindled bosom,
    the goddess   50
Comes to the home of storms, to Æolia comes,
    into regions
Teeming with furious gales. King Æolus, here,
    as dictator,
Prisons the struggling winds in the depths of a
    measureless cavern,
Curbing by chain and cell the wild and boisterous
    tempests.
Ever around their den, with an echoing moan of
    the mountain,   55
Sullenly do they roar. King Æolus, ruling with
    rigor,
Throned in his hall of state, controls them and
    tempers their fury.
But for his care, the sea and the land and the in-
    finite heavens
Surely they swiftly would sweep through the air,
    and hurl to destruction;
But the omnipotent Father hath shut them away
    in dark caverns,   60
Fearful of this, and hath set the mass of towering
    mountains
Over them there, and ordained a king, who, under
    agreement,
Knows how to hold them in check, and to give
    them free rein when commanded.

Juno, a suppliant then, to him thus made her peti-
    tion : —
" Æolus, yea, for to thee the father of gods, king
    of mortals,   65
Power hath given to quiet the waves and to raise
    them by tempests,
Sailing the Tuscan sea is a people unfriendly to
    Juno,
Troy into Italy bringing, and bringing their van-
    quished Penates.
Lash into fury thy winds, and wreck their foun-
    dering vessels !
Or disperse their fleet and scatter their bodies to
    Neptune !   70
Nymphs of the air have I, twice seven, of marvel-
    lous beauty.
Her who is fairest of all in her loveliness, Deïo-
    peia,
Firmly in wedlock to thee will I join, thine own,
    and forever,
So that with thee she may pass all her life in re-
    turn for thy favor,
Making thee also a father, and bearing thee beau-
    tiful children."   75
Æolus thus replied : " O queen, be it thine to de-
    termine
What thou desirest, and mine be the duty of doing
    thy bidding.
Sovereignty, such as I have, my kingdom, and Ju-
    piter's favor,
All are of thee, thou bidst me recline at the ban-
    quets of Heaven ;
Thou dost give me the power to govern the storm
    and the tempest."   80

When he had spoken these words, he drove the
　　cavernous mountain
In on the side with his whirling spear, and the
　　winds, like an army,
Rush where a gate is given, and sweep o'er the
　　earth in a cyclone.
East wind and South wind together, and West wind
　　burdened with tempests,
Fall on the sea, and dash it in mass from its deep-
　　est foundations,　　　　　　　　　　　　85
Rolling high on the shore great billows of turbu-
　　lent water.
Follows a shouting of men, and a whistling of
　　wind in the rigging.
Suddenly masses of cloud have robbed the eyes of
　　the Trojans
Both of the sky and the day; dark night broods
　　over the ocean;
Thunder the poles, and the heavens incessantly
　　glitter with lightning,　　　　　　　　　90
While the whole universe threatens immediate
　　death to the heroes.
Instantly icy chills unnerve the limbs of Æneas;
Groaning in spirit and stretching aloft both hands
　　to the heavens,
Thus he exclaims aloud: "O thrice and again to
　　be envied,
Ye whose fortune it was to die in the sight of the
　　fathers,　　　　　　　　　　　　　　　95
Under the lofty walls of Troy! O Diomed, bravest
Soul of the Danaan line, why was it not mine to
　　have fallen
Dead on the Ilian plain, to have yielded this life
　　to thy valor,

Where, by the lance of Achilles, fierce Hector and
    giant Sarpedon
Lie, and Simois rolls and tumbles under his bil-
    lows   100
So many shields and helms and gallant bodies of
    heroes ? "
  While he thus voices his grief, a whistling blast
    from the northward
Strikes the sail squarely in front, and raises the
    waves to the heavens.
Snapped are the oars; and adrift they roll in the
    trough of the ocean.
Heaped in confusion there follows a shuddering
    mountain of water.   105
Some hang aloft on the crest, under others the sea
    widely yawning
Lays bare its bed 'mid the surges, and sand boils
    up in the billows.
Three, by the South wind seized, are whirled upon
    reefs that lie hidden,
Rocks in the midst of the sea, in Italy known as
    The Altars,
Lifting their giant backs just out of the plane of
    the water.   110
Three by the Eastern wind are hurled from the
    deep upon sand bars;
Sad is the sight as they dash on shoals, sand heap-
    ing about them.
One ship, that which the Lycians bore, and faith-
    ful Orontes,
Full in sight of Æneas a mighty wave like a moun-
    tain
Struck on the stern, and dashed from his station
    the low-stooping pilot,   115

Hurling him headlong down ; while thrice in the
    spot where she staggered,
Whirled was the ship by the sea, and quickly de-
    voured by the whirlpool.
Now appear floating about here and there in the
    wide-circling waters
Weapons of men, and planks, and treasures of
    Troy, on the billows.
Now the stout ship of Ilioneus, now that of gallant
    Achates,   120
That in which Abas sailed, and that which bore
    aged Aletes,
All by the storm undone, and the joints of their
    sides being loosened,
Let in the hostile sea, and open in widening fis-
    sures.
    Meanwhile Neptune perceives that the sea is
    confused with an uproar ;
Sternly indignant, he sees that a storm has been
    loosed ; that the peaceful   125
Depths of the sea have been stirred ; then, looking
    forth from the ocean,
Lifts his majestic head o'er the foaming crests of
    the surges ;
Sees the fleet of Æneas dispersed far over the
    waters,
Sees the Trojans o'erwhelmed by the waves ; and
    the wreck of the heavens ;
Nor were the craft and resentment of Juno con-
    cealed from her brother.   130
Eurus and Zephyrus then he summons, and thus
    he rebukes them :
" Hath so great confidence, then, in your birth and
    your kindred possessed you

That, without sanction of mine, ye mingle the
    earth and the heavens?
And do ye dare, ye Winds, to raise these moun-
    tains of water?
Ye will I — but it were better to quiet the turbu-
    lent billows :   135
Never again for your deeds shall ye make so light
    an atonement ;
Hasten your flight, and take to your king this
    message from Neptune:
Not unto him the command of the sea and the ter-
    rible trident,
But to myself, pertain ; those desolate rocks are
    his portion,
Eurus, where thou dost dwell.   In that castle let
    Æolus bluster ;   140
There let him lord it at will o'er the winds in his
    closely barred dungeon."
Thus doth he speak ; and more quickly than words
    he hath calmed the wild waters,
Scattered the masses of cloud, and brought back
    the sun to the heavens.
Triton at once and Cymothoë, eagerly toiling to-
    gether,
Shove the ships off the sharp rock ; and Neptune
    assists with his trident,   145
Clearing great sand banks away and smoothing the
    breast of the ocean.
Then in his buoyant car he rides o'er the swell of
    the billows ;
And, as in some vast crowd, when, as often, a tu-
    mult arises,
And the ignoble throng is roused to a frenzy of
    passion,

Firebrands and stones are beginning to fly, for
　　fury finds weapons,　　　　　　　　　150
Then if they chance to behold some man revered
　　for his virtues,
Or for his faith, they are hushed, and stand in
　　breathless attention,
While he controls their hearts by his words, and
　　quiets their passions,
So all the roar of the sea hath subsided or ever the
　　Father,
Looking out over the ocean and borne under
　　brightening heavens,　　　　　　　　155
Urges his flying steeds and guides his swift chariot
　　onward.
　　Weariedly struggle the men of Æneas to pilot
　　their vessels
Each to the nearest shore, and are turned to he
　　Libyan seacoast.
Deep in a bay is an island, enclosing a harbor, and
　　spreading
Wide its protecting arms, whereon each wave from
　　the ocean　　　　　　　　　　　　160
Breaks, and divides itself into refluent curves ; and
　　beyond it,
Rising to right and left, tall cliffs and twin crags
　　threaten heaven,
Under whose sentinel summits the plain of the
　　water is silent
Far and wide ; then rises a scene of glimmering
　　woodland,
While a dark forest impends from above with
　　bristling shadow ;　　　　　　　　　165
Under the opposite front, in the hanging rocks, is
　　a grotto ;

Seats in the living rock are there, and waters of
    crystal,
Home of the nymphs; no chains here tether the
    wave-wearied vessels,
Nor with its curving beak does an anchor ever
    restrain them.
From the whole number of ships but seven re-
    main, and Æneas   170
Steals in hither with these; then the Trojans leap
    down from their galleys
With a great love for the land, and gain the cov-
    eted beaches,
Flinging their wearied limbs all dripping with
    brine on the seashore.
Quickly, however, Achates hath struck out a spark
    from a flint-stone;
Now he hath caught up the fire in leaves; dry fuel
    around it   175
He hath arranged, and now he hath kindled a
    flame in the fagots;
Then, grain, wet by the waves, and also the vessels
    for cooking,
Bring they dejectedly forth, and make ready the
    food they have rescued,
Planning to parch it with fire, and crush it with
    stones for their supper.
Meanwhile Æneas is climbing the cliff to secure
    an unbroken   180
View of the boundless deep, in the hope that some-
    thing of Antheus
Tossed by the wind he may see; some trace of the
    Phrygian galleys;
Capys, perchance, or, high on the stern, the arms
    of Caïcus.

Not one ship is in sight; but, lo, three stags that
    are straying
Down by the shore he spies; whole herds are fol-
    lowing slowly   185
After them, seeking their food in a straggling line
    through the valleys.
Here did he halt, and reach with his hand for his
    bow and his arrows
Swift of flight, for the faithful Achates was bear-
    ing these weapons.
First the leaders themselves, uplifting their heads
    and their antlers
Like tall branching trees, he drops; then the herd
    in a body   190
Driven with darts, he pursues through the leafy
    depths of the forest;
Nor does he quit the chase till seven huge bodies
    he tumbles
Victor-like to the earth, and equals the roll of his
    galleys.
Thence he returns to the harbor, and shares them
    with all his companions;
Also the wine which Acestes had kindly stored in
    their flagons   195
On the Trinacrian shore, the hero's parting re-
    membrance,
Now he divides, and he soothes by his words their
    sorrowing bosoms:
"Comrades! for this is not our first acquaintance
    with trouble,
Ye who have heavier borne, from these, too, our
    God will deliver!
Scylla's wrath ye have braved, where deep in her
    echoing cavern   200

Thundered the wave-beaten rocks; ye have also
    made trial of Cyclops
Striding among his crags; take heart, and un-
    happy foreboding
Cease; and hereafter, perhaps, to remember these
    things will be pleasant.
Through these varied disasters, through all these
    perils of fortune,
Seek we Latium still; where the Fates are dis-
    closing before us   205
Peaceful abodes; where Troy is destined to rise
    from her ashes.
Persevere, and reserve yourselves for a brighten-
    ing future."
Such were the words he spake, but his heart was
    heavy with trouble:
Hope he feigned in his face; crushed down the
    deep grief in his bosom.
Then do they gird themselves and make ready the
    deer for the banquet,   210
Tearing the hide from the ribs and exposing the
    flesh underneath it.
Some cut the meat into slices and fix it on spits,
    while it quivers;
Others set caldrons of brass on the shore and at-
    tend to the firing.
Then by the feast they renew their strength, and,
    stretched on the greensward,
Drink their fill of old wine, and feast on the fat of
    the deer-meat.   215
Then, when the tables are cleared, and their hunger
    appeased by the banquet,
Long they inquire of each other the fate of their
    missing companions,

Balancing hope and fear, half hoping they yet
    be living,
Half afraid they are dead, and beyond the
    of earth's voices.   185
Marked is the grief of kind-hearted Æneas
    inwardly sighing
Over the lot of Orontes the brave; now
    mourning:
Lycus, how cruel his fate! bold Gyas, and
    Cloanthus.
    Yet there was now an end, when Jupiter,
    in the heavens,
Looking down thence on the sail-wingèd sea
    the far stretching mainland,   190
Scanning the shores and the scattered tribes;
    throned in the heavens,
Tarried, and fixed his eyes intent on the Libya's
    kingdom.
And, as these manifold cares he is pondering there
    in his bosom,
Sorrowing more than her wont, her bright eyes
    brimming with tear-drops,
Venus entreats him thus: " O thou, who with
    endless dominion
Rulest o'er men and gods, thou, who by thy thun-
    der appallest,   200
What so great wrong hath Æneas, my son, been
    able to do thee,
What have the Trojans, to whom, after suffering
    so many death-blows,
Now the whole world, for Italy's sake, refuses a
    refuge?
Thou hast assuredly promised that hence in the far
    distant future

Thu an leaders shall rise and revive the succession
    of Teucer ;   235
Stri ng the sea and the land with universal do-
    minion.
Ceas it is the motive, my father, hath turned thee
    aside from thy purpose ?
Thr cainly I have been comforted thus for Troy's
    desolation,
Seel ighing against its pitiful ruin a happier
    future.
Pea l the same fortune pursues these victims of
    constant disaster.   240
Per ien wilt thou grant an end, Great King, unto
    these tribulations ?
Sucl not Antenor unharmed escape from the midst
    of the Grecians,
Ho read the Illyrian bays, and peacefully enter the
    inmost
Realms of Liburnia ; passing beyond the Fount of
    Timavus,
Whence, through nine great mouths, with an echo-
    ing roar of the mountain,   245
Floods burst forth and deluge the fields with thun-
    dering billows ?
There, notwithstanding, the town of Patavium he
    hath established ;
Founded a Teucrian state, and given a name to a
    nation ;
Quitted his Trojan arms, and now dwelleth in
    peace and contentment.
We, thy children, to whom thou hast promised the
    glory of heaven,   250
Ships — can I speak of it ? — lost, to gratify one
    who is angered,

We are betrayed, and far are divided from Italy i
    harbors.
This, the reward of our faith? Is it thus thou
    restorest our empire?"
Then, with that look that calms the sky and quiets
    the tempest,
Graciously smiling upon her, the father of gods
    and of mortals   255
Kisses the lips of his daughter, and answers her
    petulant chiding :
" Be not afraid, Cytherea, unchanged are the fates
    of thy people ;
Thou shalt behold Lavinium's walls and the city
    of promise,
And thou shalt bear to the stars that cluster on
    high in the heavens
Noble Æneas, and no persuasion hath altered my
    purpose.   260
This, thy son, (I will speak, for this trouble is
    preying upon thee ;
Yea, I will stir the secrets of fate, unrolling the
    future ;)
Terrible war shall wage in Italy ; peoples ferocious
Crush, and ordain for the men both laws and for-
    tified cities,
Till the third summer shall witness him ruling as
    Latium's monarch,   265
And the third winter shall bring the Rutulians
    under his sceptre.
Then this little Ascanius, taking the surname Iulus,
(Ilus it was while the Ilian state maintained its
    dominion,)
Thirty glorious years with their rolling months
    shall accomplish

There on the throne; and then transfer his domin-
    ion to Alba, 270

Leave the Lavinian realm, and build an impreg-
    nable fortress.

Here for full three hundred years shall govern-
    ment flourish

Under Hectorean kings; till at last a queen and
    a priestess,

Ilia, bride of Mars, shall bear twin sons to the
    War god.

Then, rejoiced by the tawny hide of his fostering
    wolf-nurse, 275

Romulus takes up the line and founds a war-loving
    city,

Giving his name to the state, and calling the citi-
    zens Romans.

I have determined for them nor date nor limit of
    empire;

Endless dominion I grant. Nay, even implacable
    Juno,

Who is now vexing the sea and the land and the
    sky in her terror, 280

Changed to a kindlier mood, shall join me in aid-
    ing the Romans,

Lords of the world, and the nation that robes itself
    in the toga!

Such is my pleasure. The time shall come in the
    lapse of the ages

When the Assaracan house, both noble Mycenæ
    and Phthia

Under its thrall shall bring, and reign in discom-
    fited Argos. 285

Then shall a Trojan be born of illustrious origin,
    Cæsar!

Ocean the edge of his realm, constellations the
    fringe of his glory;
Julius his name, by right of descent from mighty
/   Iulus.
Him to the heavens at last, with spoils of the
    Orient laden,
Thou shalt surely receive; and he shall be wor-
    shipped with honor.   290
Then, renouncing war, rude ages shall yield to
    refinement;
White-haired Fides and Vesta, and Remus at one
    with Quirinus,
Right shall enforce, and the gates of war, grim
    iron-bound portals,
They shall be closed and barred; behind them
    malevolent Discord,   ,
Sitting amid his engines of death, bound down by
    an hundred   295
Fetters of brass, with blood-stained lips, shall rage
    at his prison."
Thus he replies, and dispatches the son of Maia
    from Heaven
So that the lands and the newly built castles, of
    Carthage may open
Gladly to welcome the Trojans; lest Dido, with
    fate unacquainted,
Drive them away from her shore.   He flies through
    the infinite ether   300
Winging his way, and soon has alighted on Libya's
    seacoast.
Lo, his errand is done; at the will of the god the
    Phœnicians
Lay their fierceness aside, and the queen is one of
    the foremost

Kindlier thoughts to accept, and friendly good-will
    to the Trojans.

    Faithful Æneas, however, all night was uneasily
    brooding   305
Over his cares, and resolved to go forth as the
    morning was breaking,
Study the unknown land which had sheltered his
    ships from the tempest,
Learn, for he saw but a waste, whether men or
    wild beasts were its tenants,
Then, take back to his comrades a faithful report
    of the country.
Deep in a wooded cave, in the rock-sheltered arch
    of a cavern,   310
Walled about by trees and darkened by quivering
    shadows,
First he conceals his fleet; and, Achates his only
    companion,
Goes, with his hand tight clinched on his spears
    well pointed with iron.
Crossing his path in the midst of the forest, his
    mother confronts him,
Wearing a maiden's mien, and the dress and the
    arms of a maiden   315
Spartan by birth, or as Thracian Harpalyce looks
    when she wearies
Steed after steed, in her flight, and outruns the
    swift waters of Hebrus.
For she had deftly suspended a graceful bow from
    her shoulder,
Huntress-like, and her wind-tossed hair was stream-
    ing behind her.
Bare was her knee, and caught in a knot were the
    folds of her mantle.   320

Straightway she speaks: "Young men, if happily
    one of my sisters
Wandering here you have seen, pray show me the
    way she has taken,
Armed with a quiver, and girded about with a
    dark spotted lynx-hide,
Or, in full cry, in pursuit of a foam-covered boar
    through the forest."
Venus hath spoken, and thus doth Æneas reply to
    his mother :   325
" I have not heard or seen any one of thy sisters,
    O maiden ;
Maiden ! Nay, what shall I call thee? Thou
    hast not a countenance mortal,
Nor is thy voice like the voice of man. Ah, surely
    a goddess !
Art thou the sister of Phœbus ? or art thou a child
    of the wood-nymphs ?
Graciously hear us, whoever thou art, and lighten
    our trouble ;   330
Teach us beneath what sky, on what remote verge
    of the planet
We are now thrown; for, strangers alike to the
    land and the people,
Wander we, cast ashore by the wind and the moun-
    tainous billows :
Many a victim shall fall by my hand in front of
    thine altars."
Venus replied : " I consider myself unworthy such
    honor;   335
It is the habit of Tyrian maidens to carry a
    quiver,
Also the buskin of purple to bind high over the
    ankle ;

This that thou seest is Punic land, by Tyrians
    peopled ;
That is Agenor's town; fierce Libyans press on
    our borders ;
Dido is queen of the realm; she abandoned her
    Tyrian city   340
Fleeing her brother ; her wrongs to detail were
    too weary a story,
Yet I will give thee the leading events of her life
    in a moment ;
She was the bride of Sychæus, a landowner reck-
    oned the richest
Man in the city of Tyre, and devotedly loved by
    poor Dido.
Still in her maidenly bloom, her father had sanc-
    tioned their union.   345
Fair were the omens of marriage; but over the
    Tyrian people
Ruled her own brother Pygmalion, foremost in all
    that is evil.
Bitter dissension arose in the home, and by avarice
    blinded,
Disregarding his sister's love, and heaven defying,
Right at the altar he stealthily slew unsuspecting
    Sychæus.   350
Long he concealed the deed ; and feigning many a
    pretext
Basely deluded with falsehood the hope of his
    heart-broken sister.
But in her slumbers the spirit itself of her un-
    buried husband
Came, and, uplifting a face of strange and unnatu-
    ral pallor,
Showing the bloody shrine and his bosom pierced
    by the dagger,   355

Opened before her view the dark disgrace of the
    palace.
Then he persuades her to hasten her flight and
    depart from her country;
Tells of old treasure concealed in the earth to aid
    her departure,
Gold unreckoned in weight, and silver unmeasured
    in value.
Dido, aroused by this vision, made ready her flight
    and her comrades;   360
Gathered together all who detested the merciless
    tyrant,
All who were sore afraid.   Then, a vessel that
    chanced to be waiting
Seizing, they freighted with gold; and sordid Pyg-
    malion's treasure
Floated away on the sea; the head of the project,
    a woman!
Down to this place they came, where now you be-
    hold the majestic   365
Walls and rising towers of the new-born city of
    Carthage.
Next they purchased a site called Byrsa because
    of their bargain;
Only so much could they buy as their wit could
    surround with a bull's hide.
But of yourselves at last; who are you? and
    whence do ye journey?
Whither is now your course?"   To her, as she
    made these inquiries,   370
Sighing, Æneas replied, drawing speech from the
    depths of his bosom:
"Should I begin at the first, fair goddess, and fol-
    low our story,

Hadst thou also the leisure to hear the long tale
    of our trials,
Hesperus sooner would close the day, and Olympus
    be darkened.
Sailing from ancient Troy, if the name of Troy,
    peradventure,   375
Ever hath reached thine ear; through varied ex-
    panses of water,
We have been dashed on this Libyan coast by a
    freak of the tempest.
I am god-fearing Æneas; my gods from the en-
    emy rescued
Now do I bear in my fleet, and my glory is known
    in the heavens.
Italy, home, do I seek, and my birthright from
    Jove the Almighty.   380
Launching a score of ships, I embarked on the
    Phrygian waters.
Pointing the way was my mother divine, and Fate
    was my pilot.
Scarcely are seven, disabled by surges and tem-
    pests, remaining.
Poor and unknown myself, I am roaming the
    Libyan deserts,
Outcast of Europe and Asia." Venus, however,
    unable   385
Longer to bear his distress, interrupted him thus
    in his grieving:
" Whoe'er thou art, I am sure that beloved by the
    gods thou art breathing
Life-giving air, for lo! thou art come to our Tyrian
    city.
Only go forward, and hasten thy way to the gates
    of the palace;

For I announce that thy comrades are saved, that
    thy fleet hath been rescued,   390
Wafted by shifting gales to the arms of a shelter-
    ing haven,
Else have my parents instructed me vainly in vain
    divination.
Yonder twelve swans behold, in an orderly column
    exultant,
Whom, but a moment ago, Jove's eagle, down-
    swooping from heaven,
Whirled through the open sky; they now in un-
    broken procession   395
Seem to be choosing a haven, or looking on one
    they have chosen.
Now, as, in safety once more, they disport with
    their whistling pinions,
And in a company circle the sky with songs of
    rejoicing,
Even so thy ships and the youthful sailors that
    guide them
Either are safe in port, or glide with full sail into
    harbor.   400
On! then, at once, and led by this pathway, con-
    tinue thy progress."
    Speaking, she turned, and there flashed from her
    neck a roseate splendor ;
Not of the earth was the fragrance exhaled by her
    tresses ambrosial ;
Lengthening down to the earth, her robe flowed
    over her sandals,
While in her queenly step she appeared undis-
    guised, a true goddess.   405
Recognizing his mother, he cried in pursuit as she
    vanished,

"Why dost thou ever delude thy son with empty
    disguises?
Why are we never permitted to give the right
    hand to each other?
Never to hear and reply with the natural tones of
    our voices?"
Thus he upbraided his mother, and hastened his
    steps toward the city;   410
But, as they went, Venus hedged them about with
    a shadowy vapor,
Yea, did the goddess enfold them about with a
    cloud-woven mantle
So that no one might see them, nor any be able to
    touch them,
Either to cause them delay, or challenge the cause
    of their coming.
She herself, glad to revisit her home, is wafted to
    Paphos;   415
There does a temple await her, and altars an hun-
    dred are glowing
Bright with Arabian incense and fragrant with
    new-gathered garlands.
They, in the mean time, are hastening on where the
    pathway is guiding;
Already climbing the hill which, frowning far over
    the city,
Faces the towering castles that rise from the oppo-
    site valley.   420
Marvelous seem to Æneas the blocks where once
    were rude cabins;
Marvelous seem the gates, and the din, and the
    streets with their paving.
Bravely the Tyrians urge on the work; some ex-
    tending the ramparts,

Others erecting a tower, or rolling up stones for
 the builders;
Others choose sites for their homes and surround
 them with guardian furrows;   425
Laws they ordain, and judges elect, and a reverend senate.
Here again others are dredging a harbor, and others the ground-work
Deep of a theatre lay; while others hew out of
 the quarries
Columns colossal, the lofty adornment of scenes
 of the future.
Like labor urges the bees in the earliest dawning
 of summer,   430
Over bright meadows of sunshine and flowers, or
 guiding the full-grown
Young of the hive, or storing compactly the clear-
 flowing honey,
Filling their cells to o'erflowing with sweet abun-
 dance of nectar;
Some take the burdens from home-coming work-
 ers; or, forming battalions,
Drive from their precincts the drones, that idle
 and indolent faction;   435
Fervent their labor; and scented with thyme is
 the redolent honey.
"Fortunate people, the walls of whose city already are rising!"
Murmurs Æneas, uplifting his gaze to the heights
 of the city.
Then, hedged about by the cloud, he passes, O
 marvelous story!
Into the town, and mingles with men, yet no one
 perceives him.   440

There was a grove in the midst of the city, rejoi-
    cing in shadow,
Where first the Tyrians, cast on the shore by the
    waves and the tempest,
Dug up the fortunate symbol foretold by imperial
    Juno,
Even the head of a fiery steed, for so should the
    nation
Ever be famous in war, and independent for-
    ever.   445
Here Sidonian Dido was building a temple to
    Juno,
Vast, and enriched with gifts and the presence
    divine of the goddess.
Pillars of bronze arise from the steps, bronze-
    bound are the lintels,
And the huge hinges complain of the massive
    bronze of the portals.
Now, a new marvel revealed in this grove first
    lightened foreboding ;   450
Here did Æneas first venture to hope for a hap-
    pier future ;
Here first dared to look for relief from the scour-
    ging of fortune,
For, as part by part, he scans the magnificent tem-
    ple,
Waiting there for the queen, and wondering what
    lucky planet
Shone on the city, and marveling, now at the skill
    of the artists,   455
Now at their arduous toil, he sees, depicted in
    order,
Battles of Troy, and the war whose renown al-
    ready was world-wide,

Sons of Atreus, and Priam, and, cruel to both,
    stern Achilles.
Stopping abruptly, he cries with tears, "What
    place now, Achates,
What retreat on earth rings not with the fame of
    our struggle ?   460
Priam is here! even here hath worth her true guer-
    don of honor;
Grief hath her tears; and the heart is touched by
    human misfortune.
Fling away fear! our renown shall bring us a mea-
    sure of safety."
Thus he exclaimed, and his heart was cheered by
    the shadowy picture.
Groaning aloud, he drowned his face in a torrent
    of weeping;   465
For he beheld how here, where Pergamos centred
    the conflict,
Greeks were in flight, while the Trojan youth were
    hotly pursuing;
There, the Trojans were crushed by the car of
    crested Achilles.
Near by he recognized also, with tears, the pavil-
    ion of Rhesus
Spreading its snow-white vails, as, betrayed in the
    first hour of slumber,   470
Diomed, drenched with blood, defiled it with ter-
    rible slaughter,
Driving the fiery steeds to his camp or e'er they
    had tasted
Once of the pasture of Troy, or once had drunk
    from the Xanthus.
Troilus fleeing, disarmed, in another part of the
    picture,

Luckless boy, and matched in unequal strife with
    Achilles, 475
Dragged by his horses, is hanging supine from his
    riderless war-car,
Clinging still to the reins; his neck and his hair
    trail behind him
Over the earth, and scrawled is the dust by the
    spear-point inverted.
Meanwhile, matrons of Troy, their hair unbound,
    were advancing
Up to the temple of partial Minerva, and bearing
    her mantle, 480
Mournfully suppliant, beating the palms of their
    hands on their bosoms.
Pallas stood fixing her eyes on the earth, and her
    face was averted.
Thrice around Troy had Achilles been dragging
    the body of Hector;
Now he was selling for gold the lifeless form of
    his victim.
Verily then he drew a deep sigh from the depths
    of his bosom, 485
Seeing the spoils and the car, and the very body
    of Hector,
Hector his friend, and Priam outstretching his
    hands and defenseless.
Then he perceived himself engaged with the chiefs
    of the Grecians;
Also the Eastern troops, and the armor of dark-
    visaged Memnon.
Penthesilea was raging and blazed in the midst of
    her legions, 490
Leading her column of Amazons, shielded with
    glittering crescents,

Binding under her naked breast the gold of her
    girdle;
Warrior-maiden, audaciously challenging men to
    the conflict.
  While these marvellous scenes are appearing to
    Trojan Æneas,
While he is riveted there in amazement and lost
    in the vision,   495
Lo! to the temple advancing, the queen, most
    beautiful Dido,
Comes in state, with youths in a multitude throng-
    ing around her,
As by the bank of Eurotas, or over the hilltops of
    Cynthus,
Dian marshals her train, while round and about
    her a thousand
Oreads circle and dance.   But she, with her quiver
    of silver   500
Hung from her shoulder, eclipses the grace of the
    nymphs of the mountain,
While the silent heart of Latona is filled with re-
    joicing;
Such was Dido, and thus was she joyously hasten-
    ing onward,
Threading the throng, and approving the toil that
    was founding her empire.
Then, at the gates of the goddess, beneath the
    arched roof of the temple,   505
Raised aloft on her throne, 'mid a hedge of bright
    spears she is seated.
Judgment and law she ordains for the men, and
    apportions their labors,
Equaling each to the other, or trusting to chance
    the allotment,

When, on a sudden, Æneas beholds, hard pressed
    by a rabble,
Antheus drawing near with Sergestus and valiant
    Cloanthus, 510
Followed by many of those whom the dark whirl-
    ing tempest had scattered
Over the deep, and flung on other and far distant
    beaches.
Straightway Æneas was dazed, and Achates, dumb
    with amazement,
Trembled with joy and fear: for they ardently
    yearned for their comrades,
Longing to grasp their hands, but the mystery
    troubled their spirits. 515
Checking their ardor, still veiled in the cloud, they
    silently wondered
What had befallen these men; what harbor now
    sheltered their vessels;
Why they were coming; for men selected from
    each of the galleys
Came to petition for favor, and hastened with
    shouts to the temple.
When they had entered, and leave had been given
    to speak in the presence, 520
Thus, as the eldest, Ilioneus spake with his wonted
    composure:
" Gracious queen, divinely appointed to found a
    new city,
And with imperial justice to rule a proud spirited
    nation,
Trojans are we, in distress, the prey of the winds
    and the waters.
Keep, we beseech thee, the terrible peril of fire
    from our vessels; 525

Spare us, a god-fearing people, and patiently hear
    our petition.

Not with steel are we come to ravage thy Libyan
    hearthstones,

Nor to plunder thy treasure and bear it away on
    the ocean ;

We have no purpose of harm ; such presumption
    is not for the vanquished.

There is a place which is known as Hesperia,
    named by the Grecians,   530

Ancient the land, prevailing in arms, and abound-
    ing in harvests,

Settled at first by Œnotrian men ; it is said their
    descendants

Now have re-named the race from the name of their
    leader, Italian.

Thither our course was set.

When on a sudden uprose from the wave storm-
    breeding Orion,   535

Drove us on hidden shoals, and far with his south-
    ern born tempests

Scattered us over the sea, and wrecked us on rocks
    never charted.

Hither, a pitiful few, we have drifted at last to thy
    harbor.

What is this race of men ? What country so bar-
    barous is it

Sanctions behavior like this ? The refuge of sand
    is denied us ;   540

Quarrels are sought, nay, we are forbidden to step
    on thy borders.

E'en though ye fear not man, though ye hold mor-
    tal arms in derision,

Yet of the gods beware, who are mindful of good
    and of evil.

There was a ruler among us, Æneas, and none was
    more upright,
None more devoted, nor any more mighty in arms
    or in battle.   545
This man, if fate hath preserved, if still he is liv-
    ing and breathing
Heaven-born air, nor already lies low in the pitiless
    shadows,
We shall not fear, nor will any advances of timely
    assistance
Cause thee regret.   There are cities, moreover, in
    Sicily's confines,
Cities and fields, and of Trojan progenitors, kingly
    Acestes.   550
Grant us permission to land our storm-shaken
    boats on thy beaches,
Timbers to hew in thy forests, and oars to trim for
    our galleys;
So that if Italy call us, if comrades and king be
    recovered,
Italy, then, we may joyfully seek and Latium's
    harbor;
But, if our safety be slain; if thee, O best father
    of Trojans,   555
Libyan waters are holding; if now we despair of
    Iulus;
Yet, even then, to Sicanian harbors and homes
    that await us,
We may retrace our way, and seek a new king in
    Acestes."
Thus did Ilioneus plead, and the Dardans, all
    shouting together,
Thundered applause.   560
Dido, then, with downcast eyes, spake briefly in
    answer:

"Teucrians, fear from your hearts set free; put
away apprehension;
Trouble and newness of kingdom compel these
unfriendly precautions,
Force me with sentinels widely extended to guard
my dominions
Men of Æneas, the city of Troy! Who is igno-
rant of them?   565
Or of the deeds and the men and the flames of a
war so tremendous?
Not so hardened the hearts we Carthaginians
carry;
Nor doth the sun yoke his horses so far from our
Tyrian city;
Whether ye choose Hesperia's broad Saturnian
cornfields,
Whether ye choose the borders of Eryx, and
kingly Acestes,   570
I will dismiss you in safety with escorts, and lend
you assistance.
Yet, are ye willing, as equals, to stay with me
here in my kingdom?
Lo, then, the town I am building is yours; I will
harbor your vessels;
Trojan and Tyrian, I am your queen, I will make
no distinction.
Yet do I wish that your king, compelled by the
same southern tempest,   575
Also were with us, Æneas himself! I will send
through my seacoasts
Trustworthy men, and command them to search
through the Libyan borders;
Shipwrecked, he still may be straying in some of
our forests or cities."

Stirred in soul by these words, brave Achates and
    father Æneas
Long had been burning to break from the cloud
    that hung darkly around them.   580
Nor did Achates forbear to address the first word
    to Æneas :
" Child of a goddess ! what thoughts are surging
    now in thy bosom ?
All thou beholdest safe ; thy fleet and thy friends
    are recovered.
One is not here, whom we, with our eyes beheld as
    he perished,
Drowned in the sea ; all else is fulfilling the words
    of thy mother."   585
Scarcely had this been said, when suddenly, lo,
    the encircling
Cloud divided itself, and dissolved in invisible
    vapor.
Then in clear light was Æneas revealed, and he
    stood forth resplendent,
Godlike in face and form ; for with radiant hair
    had his mother
Crowned her son ; and over him breathed youth's
    roseate splendor,   590
Kindling in his eyes the glory of beauty and glad-
    ness ;
Glory such as to ivory art may add, or when
    silver,
Or white Parian marble, with yellow gold is sur-
    rounded.
Suddenly then, unexpected by all, the queen he
    addresses :
" I, whom thou seekest, am here ! Behold me in
    person before thee !   595

Trojan Æneas, snatched from the jaws of Libyan
    breakers!
Thou, who alone dost compassionate Troy's un-
    speakable sorrows,
Thou, who hast taken us, left by Greeks, and worn
    out by disasters
Both of the land and sea, all destitute, into thy
    city,
Into thy home, to return an acknowledgment
    worthy, O Dido,   600
This is not in our power, nor yet in the power of
    whatever
Remnant of Teucrian men may be scattered abroad
    on this planet;
But may the gods, if any divinities care for the
    righteous,
If ever justice avail, or a heart that is conscious
    of virtue,
Recompense fitting vouchsafe thee! what age so
    gladsome hath borne thee!   605
Who are the parents so great have begotten so
    noble a daughter!
Long as the rivers shall run to the sea; as long
    as the shadows
Circle the slopes of the mountains, and stars are
    nurtured in heaven,
Ever thy glory, forever thy name and thy praise
    shall continue,
Be where it may our home!" He paused, and
    Ilioneus warmly   610
Welcoming with his right, with his left hand he
    greeted Serestus,
Then all the others, both Gyas, the valiant, and
    valiant Cloanthus.

First, by the strange apparition was Tyrian Dido
    astounded,
Then by the man's great grief, and then her lips
    moved, and she answered :
"What is the fate that through peril so terrible,
    child of a goddess,   615
Follows thee on ? What pow'r to these desolate
    shores hath constrained thee ?
Art thou indeed that Æneas, begotten by Dardan
    Anchises,
Borne by the Queen of Love where Phrygian
    Simois floweth ?
Yet I remember now that Teucer once visited
    Sidon,
Banished his father's realm, and looking about
    for another   620
Kingdom with Belus to aid; Father Belus was
    sweeping with havoc
Cypria's fruitful fields, and ruling by virtue of
    conquest.
Ever since then have I known of the fates that
    have shadowed thy city,
Known of the name of Troy, thy name and the
    kings of the Grecians.
This very prince, though a foe, held the Teucrians
    greatly in honor,   625
Proud that he too was derived from the ancient
    stock of the Teucri :
Wherefore, arise, O youths ! and accompany us to
    our palace.
Fortunes akin to yours have decreed that I also
    must settle
In this land at last, after passing through manifold
    trials ;

Not unacquainted with grief, I am learning to aid
    the unhappy."   630

Thus she speaks, and leads Æneas at once to the
    palace,

While she ordains for the shrines of the gods ap-
    propriate honors,

Not forgetting the while to dispatch to the shore
    for his comrades

Twenty bulls and the bristling backs of an hun-
    dred enormous

Swine, and she added an hundred fatling lambs
    with their mothers,   635

Bountiful gifts for the day.

Ah, but her home within, with regal magnificence
    furnished,

Dazzles the eye, and a banquet is laid in the midst
    of the palace;

Draperies wrought with art, and colored with cost-
    liest purple,

Massive plate on the tables, of silver, embossed
    with ancestral   640

Deeds of valor, in gold; a long, long history,
    stretching

Through such a number of men, from the far dis-
    tant source of her kindred.

    Now doth Æneas, whose fatherly love disquiets
    his spirit,

Bid swift-footed Achates run down at full speed
    to the harbor,

Tell Ascanius all, and bring the boy back to the
    city.   645

All the affectionate father's care in Ascanius
    centres.

Gifts, moreover, he bids him bring, from Ilium's
    ruins

Snatched in their flight; a robe, with golden em-
 broidery stiffened;

Also a veil that is woven around with yellow acan-
 thus;

Ornaments these of Helen of Argos, the same she
 had carried   650

Out of Mycenæ when seeking in Troy an unhal-
 lowed alliance;

They were the wondrous wedding gifts of Leda,
 her mother.

There was the sceptre, too, which Ilione formerly
 carried,

First born daughter of Priam; and there was a
 marvelous necklace

Lustrous with pearls, and a golden tiara resplendent with jewels.   655

Hast'ning for these, was Achates now speeding his
 way to the vessels.

 But Cytherea new plots and plans in her heart
 is devising,

That, with appearance changed, and changed in
 countenance, Cupid,

Rather than charming Ascanius, come, and en-
 kindle the frenzied

Queen with his gifts, and entwine with fire the
 heart in her bosom,   660

For she distrusts the race, fears the double-tongued
 people of Carthage,

Terrible Juno affrights her, and trouble returns
 with the nightfall.

Therefore she makes her appeal to Cupid, the
 wing-bearing love-god:

"Son, my reliance, in whom alone my mastery
 dwelleth,

Thou who laughest when Jupiter's thunder ap-
    palleth the mighty,   665
Thou art my refuge.   I humbly invoke thy divine
    intervention.
How thy brother Æneas is driven about ev'ry sea-
    coast
Over the deep by the hatred and cruel injustice of
    Juno;
This is well known to thee; thou hast ever been
    grieved by my sorrow.
Him, Carthaginian Dido detains, and with gentle
    entreaty   670
Hinders too long, and I dread these kindly atten-
    tions of Juno
How they may turn, for she in a crisis so great
    will not slumber.
Wherefore I plan to prevent her by guile; and
    the queen to encompass
Close with the fires of love, that, unmoved by the
    will of the goddess,
She may be bound to me by her passionate love
    for Æneas.   675
How canst thou bring this about?   Attend, while
    I tell thee my purpose.
He, my chiefest concern, the Prince, is preparing
    to hasten,
Called by his father's love to enter the Tyrian
    city,
Bearing gifts that are left from the sea and Troy's
    conflagration;
Him will I lull to sleep, and hide in my sacred
    pavilion,   680
High on Idalia's mountain or on the high hills of
    Cythera,

So that he neither can know my designs nor un-
consciously thwart them.

Thou for one night, not more, must deceptively
copy his likeness,

And, a boy thyself, take the boy's familiar appearance,

So that when close to her side, rejoicingly, Dido
shall place thee, 685

At the imperial board all bright with the flashing
of wine-cups,

When in her arms she shall fold thee and press
tender kisses upon thee,

Thou shalt a hidden flame inspire, and betray her
with poison.''

Cupid obeys the behest of his cherishing mother,
and pinions

Doffing, sets off with rejoicing, assuming the step
of Iulus. 690

Then doth Venus diffuse through the limbs of
Ascanius peaceful

Sleep; yea, lulled in her bosom the goddess doth
carry him gently

Up to her lofty Idalian groves, where marjoram
softly

Wraps him about with flowers and a fragrant
coolness of shadow.

Lo, now, obeying her words, and bearing the
offerings regal, 695

Cupid was seeking the city, delighted to follow
Achates.

When he appeared, the queen was already com-
posed on her golden

Couch, with its tapestry royal, and placed in the
centre of honor.

Enters now Father Æneas; and now the young
    Trojans assemble,
Ranging themselves at the board, and reclining on
    couches of purple. 700
Water is given by slaves for their hands; bread
    offered in baskets;
Napkins also are brought of smooth and delicate
    finish.
Handmaidens fifty within; their care to make
    ready the viands, —
Long the array, — and with kindling fires to honor
    the hearth-gods.
Others an hundred, and pages as many, all equally
    youthful, 705
Burden the tables with dainties, and set out the
    glittering goblets;
Nor do the Tyrians fail to throng the welcoming
    doorways,
Greet one another, and bidden, recline on the tap-
    estried couches.
All are surprised by the gifts of Æneas; sur-
    prised by Iulus,
Won by the sparkling eyes of the god, and the
    rogue's pretty speeches; 710
Pleased by the robe, and the veil embroidered
    with yellow acanthus.
Chiefest of all, unhappy Phœnissa, foredoomed to
    destruction,
Cannot appease her heart, and kindles anew while
    she gazes,
Strangely moved by the boy, and equally touched
    by the presents.
When he has run to the arms and clung to the
    neck of Æneas, 715

Satisfying his love and roguishly calling him fa-
    ther,
Cupid runs to the queen.   Her eyes are riveted on
    him ;
Riveted all her soul ; and she presses him oft to
    her bosom,
Little aware, poor Dido, how mighty a god was in
    ambush.
He, to his mother true, with the thought of effa-
    cing Sychæus,   720
Little by little begins to arouse by a living affec-
    tion
Thoughts that have slumbered long, and a heart
    long unwonted to passion.   .
\ When the first lull in the banquet is come, and
    cleared are the tables,
Generous bowls are set, and the wine is encircled
    with garlands.
Then there 's a clash in the hall, and voices ring
    out through the palace ;   725
Down from the gold-fretted ceilings, radiant lamps
    are suspended.
Darkness is put to flight by the flaring flame of
    the torches.
Then calls the queen for her bowl ; it is heavy with
    gold and with jewels.
Fills with wine the cup which Belus and all after
    Belus
Ever were wont to use ; then silence is made in the
    palace.   730
" Jupiter, for we are taught that thou guardest
    the host and the stranger,
Grant that this day may be bright to the Tyrians,
    bright to the Trojans ;

Grant that our children's children may hold it
    long in remembrance.
Be with us, Bacchus, thou giver of joy; good
    Juno be with us.
Tyrians! cheers for this union, and here's to the
    health of our guest-friends."   735
Dido hath spoken, and sprinkled the table with
    sparkling libation.
Then first lightly she touched her lips to the brim
    of the goblet,
Passing it next to Bitias, calling his name with a
    challenge;
Quaffs he in haste from the foaming cup, yea,
    drinks from the brimming
Bowl; and the princes beyond in turn. Then long-
    haired Iopas   740
Plays on a cithern of gold as Atlas, the mighty,
    hath taught him;
Sings of the wandering moon, and sings of the
    sun and eclipses,
Whence the race of man and beast, whence rain
    and the lightning,
Sings of the Hyades stormy, and sings of the
    Bears and Arcturus,
Sings why the wintry sun so hastens to dip in the
    ocean,   745
Sings why summer nights are delayed so long in
    their coming.
Tyrians thunder applause, and Trojans reëcho
    their plaudits.
Meanwhile was Dido, unhappy, protracting the
    night with a tangled
Web of discourse, and drinking long draughts
    from the deep cup of passion;

Having so much to inquire about Priam; so much
    about Hector; 750
Now, with what armor the son of Aurora had
    come to the battle,
Now, what horses had Diomed; now, how great
    was Achilles.
" Nay, good guest," she cries, " be pleased to tell
    us the story
From the very beginning, the plots of the Gre-
    cians, thy trials,
And thy wandering course; for the seventh sum-
    mer already 755
Bears thee on land astray, and bears thee adrift
    on the ocean."

BOOK II

ALL became silent, uplifting their faces in eager
    attention.
Then, from his lofty couch, spake Father Æneas
    as follows :
"Thou dost require me, O queen, to revive an
    unspeakable sorrow,
How the dominion of Troy, and the mournful
    realm of the Trojans,
Greeks overthrew ; all the heartrending scenes I
    have witnessed, nay even   5
Great part of which I have been. In relating so
    grievous a story,
Who of the Myrmidon tribe, what soldier of cruel
    Ulysses,
Or of Dolopia's army, could keep back the tears?
    and already
Damp night rushes in haste from the sky, and
    the planets declining
Summon to sleep. But if thou art so eager to
    learn our misfortunes,   10
If thou wouldst briefly be told Troy's final and
    desperate struggle ;
Though I may shrink from the pain, though shud-
    ders my soul to remember,
I will begin. Defeated in battle and baffled by
    fortune,
Year after year still slipping away, by divine in-
    spiration,

Prompted by Pallas, the chiefs of the Greeks
    built a horse, that in stature   15
Equaled a mountain, its ribs interweaving with
    planks of the fir-tree.
Pledged for a safe return, they pretended; that
    rumor was published.
Stalwart men, selected with care, they stealthily
    prisoned
Deep in its gloomy flank, and filled were its hid-
    den recesses,
Hollow and huge, and its paunch, with soldiers in
    glittering armor.   20
    Tenedos, plainly in sight, is an island exceed-
    ingly famous,
Teeming with wealth as long as the kingdom of
    Priam continued,
Now it is only a bay, and a harbor distrusted by
    vessels.
Hither conveyed, they secreted themselves on the
    desolate seashore.
We believed them gone, yes, flown with the winds
    to Mycenæ;   25
Therefore all Teucria breaks the long bondage of
    sorrow and mourning.
Gates flung wide, what joy to go out to the Do-
    rian camp-ground,
View the deserted plain, and gaze on the beaches
    forsaken.
Here, the Dolopian band, there, savage Achilles
    had tented;
Here they had moored their fleet, and yonder had
    marshaled for battle.   30
Part of us stare at the ominous gift of unwedded
    Minerva,

Dazed by the bulk of the horse; and first Thy-
     mœtes exhorts us :
‘Bring it within the walls, in the citadel give it a
     station.’
Traitor! or already thus were tending the fates of
     the Trojans.
Capys, however, and they whose minds were of
     clearer discernment,   35
Bade us precipitate into the sea all the craft of
     the Grecians,
All their insidious gifts, or kindle a fire and de-
     stroy them ;
Or, bore into the side and explore the deep lair of
     the belly.
Thus is the wavering throng divided in contrary
     factions.
First before all of them there, with a multitude
     crowding behind him,   40
Down from the citadel’s height Laocoön angrily
     hastens,
Crying afar, ‘Alas, poor countrymen, what is this
     folly ?
Think ye the enemy gone ?   Believe ye still there
     are any
Gifts of the Greeks untainted with guile ? Is
     Ulysses forgotten ?
Either enclosed in this timber Achæans are lurk-
     ing in ambush,   45
Or the machine is an engine upreared in the face
     of our ramparts,
Built to command our homes, and prepared to
     descend on our city ;
Or there is still some plot ; trust not in the horse,
     O ye Trojans !

Be what it may, even paying their vows, I'm
    afraid of the Grecians.'
Thus having spoken, he hurled a great spear with
    his powerful muscles   50
Into the creature's side and the jointed curve of
    the belly.
Quivering there it stuck, and jarred was the horse
    to the centre;
Thundered its cavernous flanks, and rumbled its
    echoing hollows.
Then, if the fates of the gods, and our judgment
    had not been perverted,
He had compelled us to spoil with steel the lair of
    the Argives,   55
Troy, thou wouldst yet remain, and thou, lofty
    fortress of Priam!
Lo, at this moment, some shepherds of Troy, with
    tumult and shouting,
Drag to the king a youth whose hands are pinioned
    behind him.
He, of his own accord, had surrendered himself,
    though a stranger,
Crossing their path for the purpose of opening
    Troy to the Grecians.   60
Daring in heart was he; for either alternative
    ready,
Either to work out the plot, or yield to sure death
    if discovered.
Eddying round on every side in a struggle to see
    him
Jostle the Trojan youth, and vie in deriding the
    captive.
Hearken ye now to the wiles of the Greeks, and
    from one act of treason,   65

Learn the whole race.

For as he stood in full view of the throng, defense-
    less and troubled,

Gazing around with his eyes on the cordon of
    Phrygian soldiers,

' Ah !' he exclaimed, ' what land, what sea can now
    yield me a refuge ?

Wretch that I am, what now is left me at last for
    my portion ?   70

Nowhere remaineth for me any place among Greeks,
    and the Trojans,

Yea, they also in wrath the atonement of blood are
    demanding.'

Changed was our mood by his grief, and checked
    was each rude demonstration.

Then we exhort him to speak, to say of what blood
    are his kindred,

Tell what news he may bring, what confidence
    claim as a captive.   75

Finally, laying aside his fear, he answered as fol-
    lows :

' Happen what may, O king, I will surely acknow-
    ledge before thee

All that is true,' he cried, ' nor deny my descent
    from the Argives ;

This at the first ; nor although a malevolent For-
    tune hath rendered

Sinon so wretched, not yet shall she render him
    false or deceitful.   80

If, peradventure, by rumor, the name Palamedes
    Belides

Ever hath come to thine ear, or the widespreading
    fame of his glory,

Him, under false accusation, though innocent,
    wickedly slandered,

Guilty alone of opposing the war, the Pelasgians
    murdered ;

Now that he lies in the darkness of death, too late
    they deplore him.   85

He was my comrade and kin, and with him my
    impoverished father

Sent me off to the war in the earliest years of
    young manhood.

While he stood high in the state and strong in the
    council of princes,

I, too, had some reputation, and carried a measure
    of honor.

Afterward, when through the envy of ever deceit-
    ful Ulysses —   90

I am betraying no secret — he passed from the
    shores of the living,

Broken in spirit, I fretted my life with gloomy
    repining,

Deeply resenting in heart the fate of my innocent
    comrade ;

Nor did I hold my peace, but foolishly vowed that,
    if Fortune

Ever should guide my victorious feet to my people
    in Argos,   95

I would avenge his death; my words aroused bit-
    ter resentment.

Thence my ruin began ; thereafter forever Ulysses

Kept me in fear by new charges, and scattered
    mysterious whispers

Over the camp, and constantly sought a conspira-
    tor's weapons ;

Nor, in fact, did he rest until, Calchas abetting his
    purpose, —-   100

Yet, after all, why vainly rehearse this harrowing
    story ?

Wherefore delay, if ye hold all Greeks at the
    same valuation?

If ye have heard enough; postpone your vengeance
    no longer;

This would the Ithacan wish; the Atridæ repay
    with a fortune.'

Then were we truly impatient to hear and consider
    his pleading;   105

Strangers to crime so base; unversed in Pelasgian
    cunning.

Faltering he proceeds, and speaks from his treach-
    erous bosom:

'Often the Greeks, out-worn by the ever-length-
    ening conflict,

Longed to effect a retreat, leave Troy, and return
    to Achaia;

Would they had done it! As often, the terrible
    wrath of the ocean   110

Intercepted their flight, and a southern-born tem-
    pest dismayed them.

Notably, just as this horse, compacted with timbers
    of maple,

Rose to its feet, the whole firmament echoed with
    warnings of thunder.

Anxiously then to the temple of Phœbus Eury-
    palus hastens;

These are the grievous words he brings from the
    shrine of Apollo: 115

'It was with blood ye appeased the winds, and
    the death of a virgin,

When at the first ye came, O Greeks, to the Ilian
    seacoast;

It is with blood ye must seek return; by the life
    of a Grecian

Ye must appease the gods ; ' this rumor filled the
    encampment.

Then were our minds benumbed, and a tremor of
    chill apprehension   120

Thrilled our hearts. Who was summoned by
    Fate ? Who called by Apollo ?

Then did the Ithacan drag to the front with a
    mighty commotion

Calchas, the soothsayer, fiercely demanding the
    oracle's meaning.

Even then there were many who warned me against
    the impostor's

Merciless crime; and many in silence foresaw
    what was coming.   125

Twice five days he is dumb, discreetly refusing to
    sentence

One by his priestly lips ; or one to single for
    slaughter.

Finally, fairly forced by the Ithacan's violent
    urging,

Playing his part, he speaks, and designates me for
    the altar.

All were content, and the fate that each for him-
    self had been dreading   130

Bore with composure when turned to the death of
    another less happy.

Dawns the accursed day ; prepared are my sacred
    adornments ;

Strewn is the salted meal ; the fillets are crowning
    my temples.

Death I have robbed of his prey; I confess it; I
    broke from my fetters,

And, in a marshy lake, all night I lay hid in the
    rushes   135

Anxiously watching to catch the first gleam of a
    sail on the water.
Now, no more can I hope to behold the old land of
    my childhood,
Look on my children dear, or return to my father
    belovéd;
Whom they will even (it may be) demand by
    way of atonement
Now I have fled, and avenge this fault by their
    pitiful slaughter.   140
Now, by the gods above, by spirits omniscient and
    holy,
By, — if there be any yet remaining on earth
    among mortals, —
By an inviolate faith, I beseech thee compassionate
    trials
Grievous as mine, and be gracious to one so un-
    justly afflicted.'
  Life for his tears we grant, and freely we give
    him our pity.   145
Priam himself at first commands that his shackles
    be loosened,
Loosened his chafing cords; and thus addresses
    him kindly:
'Give up the Greeks henceforth, whoever thou art,
    and forget them.
Be one of us; yet answer exactly the questions I
    ask thee.
Why have they reared this bulk of a monstrous
    horse? Who its author?   150
What do they seek? What rite of religion?
    What engine of warfare?'
So spake the king; and the stranger, well skilled
    in Pelasgian cunning,

Stretching his hands released from the cords aloft
    to the heavens:
' Witness ye, deathless fires, ye spirits inviolate,
    witness,
Witness,' he cries, ' ye terrible blades and altars
    unhallowed   155
I have escaped; ye fillets divine that I wore as a
    victim;
May I not rightly abjure the sacred oaths of the
    Grecians,
Rightly abhor the men, and bring to the light all
    their secrets
Should there be any concealed?   I am bound by
    no laws of my country.
Only do thou, O Troy, abide by thy word, and
    when rescued,   160
Keep thou thy faith, if I bring thee true tidings
    and amply requite thee.
All the hope of the Greeks, all faith in the war
    from the outset,
Ever hath rested in Pallas; but Pallas befriends
    them no longer;
For, since Diomed vile, and Ulysses, the plotter
    of evil,
Ventured to tear from its consecrate temple the
    form of Minerva,   165
Fatal Palladium, slaying the guards on the height
    of her fortress,
Seized the image divine, and rudely assaulted the
    goddess,
Daring with blood-stained hands to defile her im-
    maculate fillets,
Ever since then have the hopes of the Greeks been
    failing and falling;

Broken has been their might, estranged the heart
    of the goddess.   170
Nor with uncertain signs did Tritonia show her
    displeasure ;
Scarce was the image lodged in the camp when
    glittering flashes
Blazed from her angry eyes, and briny sweat be-
    · gan coursing
Down her limbs, and thrice from the earth, I tell
    it with wonder,
Leaped the statue itself, with shield and quivering
    sceptre.   175
Instantly Calchas declares that now we must flee
    o'er the ocean,
Tells us that Pergamos cannot be razed by the
    swords of the Argives
If they repeat not the omens at Argos, and bring
    back the goddess
Whom they have carried away o'er the deep in
    their high curving galleys.
Now that, borne by the wind, they have flown to
    their native Mycenæ,   180
Arms they prepare, and gods to befriend, and, re-
    crossing the water,
Suddenly they will be here.   Thus Calchas inter-
    prets the omens.
Heeding the warning, this horse they have built in
    place of the image,
Built for the injured god, to atone for their im-
    pious outrage.
Calchas, however, ordained that this towering mass
    be erected,   185
Knit with timbers of oak, and lifted high to the
    heavens,

So that it never might pass your gates, nor enter
    your city,
Nor your people protect by the shield of their an-
    cient religion.
For, if your hands affront the gifts that are vowed
    to Minerva,
Then great ruin — on him may the gods rather
    visit the omen ! —   190
Surely shall fall on the kingdom of Priam and all
    of you Trojans ;
But, if beneath your hands it ascend to the heights
    of your city,
Asia, unprovoked, shall come with her legions to
    Argos,
And upon us and ours this curse shall be fastened
    forever.'
Through such treacherous words, and the art of
    perjuring Sinon,   195
Credence was given the tale ; and we were en-
    snared by devices,
Trapped by treacherous tears, whom Diomed never
    had conquered,
Nor Larissæan Achilles, a decade, nor thousands
    of warships.
  Here something other and greater, and far more
    fitted to frighten,
Happened to us, and filled with dismay our un-
    prepared bosoms.   200
Priestly Laocoön, chosen by lot for the service of
    Neptune,
Chanced a huge bull to be slaying in front of the
    consecrate altar.
Lo, twin serpents from Tenedos, over the motion-
    less water, —

Still do I shudder to tell it, — writhing in huge
    undulations,
Burden the sea, and side by side, to the shore are
    advancing.   205
See! 'mid the surf their breasts are erect, and
    their terrible blood-red
Crests command the waves, while the hinder part
    of their bodies
Sweeps through the sea, and their giant backs are
    coiling in spirals.
Now there's a sound in the seething brine: now
    they glide to the seashore;
Tinged with blood and with fire, their eyes are an-
    grily blazing,   210
While with their flickering tongues their hissing
    lips they are licking.
Pale, we flee from the sight; but they, in a course
    undeflected,
Rush on Laocoön; then, at first, each serpent sur-
    rounding
One of his sons with its coils, embraces his delicate
    body,
Tearing the limbs with its teeth, and mangling the
    pitiful morsels.   215
Then himself, rushing up to their aid, and bearing
    his weapons,
Seizing, they bind with their spirals huge; and
    when they have circled
Doubly about his waist, and doubly his throat
    have enfolded
Close with their scale-clad breasts, their heads and
    long necks rise above him.
Then with both his hands he strains at the knots
    that enclose him;   220

Dyed are his fillets with blood, and blackened by
    splashes of venom ;

Frightful shrieks he utters the while, appealing to
    heaven ;

Roars like the wounded bull, that, breaking away
    from the altar,

Angrily shakes from his neck the axe that wavered
    in falling.

But the two dragons have glided away to the
    height of the temple ;   225

Lo, they are seeking in flight the shrine of relent-
    less Minerva ;

Now, at her very feet, by the orb of her shield are
    they sheltered.

Then indeed through each trembling heart steals
    fresh trepidation ;

Then it is whispered about that Laocoön justly
    hath suffered

Punishment for his crime, in that with the point
    of his weapon   230

He hath dishonored the sacred oak, with his im-
    pious iron

Piercing its breast; all cry : ' Let the image be
    brought to the temple !

Heaven's forgiveness invoked.'

Then, dividing the ramparts, we open the walls of
    our city ;

All are girded for work, arranging the gliding of
    rollers   235

Under its feet, while cables of hemp they attach to
    the shoulders.

Lo, the engine of death with its burden of soldiers
    in armor

Crosses the walls, while around it our boys and in-
    nocent maidens

Carol their sacred hymns and joyously tug at the
    cable.

Still it advances, and, threatening, glides to the
    heart of the city.   240

Country of mine! O, Ilium, home of the gods!
    and ye Trojan

Bulwarks famous in war! four times at the gate's
    very threshold

Halting it stopped; four times from within came
    a rattling of armor;

Nevertheless, we continue, unheeding, and blind
    in our madness,

Till in our holy tower we have lodged the calami-
    tous monster.   245

Then Cassandra, too, unsealed with a song of the
    future

Lips, by command of Apollo, forever unheeded by
    Trojans.

We, poor wretches, for whom that day should have
    no to-morrow,

Covered the shrines of the gods with garlands of
    joy through the city.

    Meanwhile the sky was revolving, and Night,
        rushing up from the ocean,   250

Folded around with shadows vast the earth and
    the heavens,

Hiding the Myrmidon wiles; the Trojans, dis-
    persed through the city,

All became silent; their limbs, overwearied, close
    pinioned by slumber.

Yet already the Grecian host, their boats in a
    column,

Soon as the stern of the royal ship had flashed up
    the signal,   255

Bound for the well-known shores of Troy, from
    Tenedos loosing,

On through the friendly hush of the silent moon
    were advancing.

Meanwhile Sinon, secure in the partial favor of
    heaven,

Stealthily loosens the bars of pine and releases the
    Grecians.

Yawning, the horse gives them back to the air;
    from the dark oaken hollow   260

Gladly they press, Thessandrus and Sthenelus
    leading, and Thoas,

Acamas, too, and Ulysses, all gliding down on a
    lowered

Rope; Neoptolemus, grandson of Peleus; though
    first was Machāon,

Then Menelaüs, and lastly Epeus, who framed the
    imposture.

Now they steal through the town, deep buried in
    wine and in slumber;   265

Now are the guards cut down, and, the gates flying
    open, they welcome

All their companions and friends, and join their
    confederate forces.

    It was the time when sleep, God's gift to his suf-
    fering children,

First begins, and silently steals full sweetly upon
    them.

Fronting my eyes in dreams, behold, most sorrow-
    ful Hector   270

Seems to be standing before me; his tears are
    falling in torrents;

Just as of yore when bound to the car, and dark
    with the bloody

Dust; his feet pierced through; and rankling with
    thongs of leather.
Ah, my heart, what a sight! Alas, how changed
    from that Hector
Proudly returning from war, adorned with the
    * spoils of Achilles;   275
Or, as on Grecian ships he hurled his Phrygian
    fire-brands!
Stiff was his beard with blood; blood-stiffened the
    locks on his forehead;
Bearing those numberless wounds, which under
    the walls of his country
He had received. Then weeping myself, I seemed
    to upbraid him;
Fain to express with my voice the distress that
    burdened my bosom: 280
'O thou light of Dardania; surest hope of the
    Trojans,
Why dost thou come so late? From what far
    country, my Hector,
Comest thou, waited long? Alas, that worn and
    discouraged,
Only now we behold thee, when hosts of thy com-
    rades have fallen!
After the manifold woes of war and our town!
    What unworthy   285
Cause hath disfigured the calm of thy face? Why
    comest thou wounded?'
Naught he replied, nor at all did he heed my idle
    inquiries;
Gravely drawing instead a groan from the depth
    of his bosom,
'Ah, thou child of a goddess,' he said, 'escape
    from these burnings!

Enemies hold the walls ; Troy falls from her proud
    elevation !   290
Now for our country and Priam, enough hath been
    done ; if our city
Could have been saved by the hand of man, my
    hand would have saved it ;
Troy entrusts unto thee her sacred rites and her
    hearth-gods ;
Take them to share thy fate, for them seek a wide-
    spreading city,
Which, after roaming the sea, thou shalt finally
    build in their honor.'   295
Ceasing, he brings with his hands the fillets, and
    powerful Vesta,
Also the deathless fire from the innermost shrine
    of her chapel.
Meanwhile in every part is the city commingled in
    mourning ;
Clearer and still more clear, though the home of
    my father Anchises
Stands remote and sheltered by trees, retired from
    the highway,   300
Sounds are distinguished, and rushes upon us the
    rumble of battle.
Then do I start from my slumber, and, clambering
    up to the turret,
Mount to the roof, and, standing erect, attentively
    listen ;
Just as when over a wheat-field a flame with a
    furious tempest
Rushes along, or with mountain-born flood an im-
    petuous torrent   305
Levels the fields, and the harvest glad, and the
    labors of oxen,

Headlong dragging the groves, a shepherd, at loss
 for its meaning,
Catching the sound from his rocky height, stands
 mute and bewildered.
Then, indeed, flashes the truth into light, and the
 plots of the Grecians
Dawn on our minds; and, now, Deiphobus' wide-
 spreading palace,   310
Vanquished by fire, is wrecked; Ucalegon blazes
 beside it;
While the broad straits of Sigeum are gleaming
 afar in the firelight.
Rises a clamor of men; an alarum is sounded by
 trumpets;
Arms, in my folly, I seize, nor in arms have I
 needful discretion.
Yet is my heart on fire to assemble a band for the
 conflict,   315
And with my comrades rush on to the citadel;
 fury and anger
Sweep me along, and I dream of the glory of dying
 in battle.
Panthus, too, behold, escaped from the spears of
 the Argives,
Panthus Othryades, priest of the citadel, priest of
 Apollo,
Temple service, and vanquished gods, and one little
 grandson   320
Dragging unaided, and rushing distractedly up to
 my doorway.
' Where is the brunt of the battle, O Panthus?
 What tow'r are we taking?'
Scarce had I spoken thus, when he sighed, and
 returned me this answer:

'Troy's last day has come, and the irresistible
    moment;
Trojans we were, Troy was, and the grandeur of
    Teucrian glory!   325
Pitiless Jupiter now hath transferred all his favor
    to Argos;
Now in a city of flame the Greeks are ruling tri-
    umphant;
Tow'ring aloft in the heart of the city, the horse
    is outpouring
Soldiers in arms, and victorious Sinon insultingly
    scatters
Fire as he goes; while others crowd in as the gates
    are thrown open,   330
Thousands as many as ever have come from mighty
    Mycenæ.
Some have already beset with their weapons the
    narrowing highways,
Blocking the streets; an array of serried and glit-
    tering spear-points
Stands with a threat of death; scarce venture the
    guards at the gateway
Battle at first, and resist in a blind and disorderly
    struggle.'   335
Then, by the will of the gods, and the words by
    Othryades spoken,
Into the flames and the fight I am borne, whither
    gloomy Erinys,
Whither the uproar calls; and clamor arises to
    heaven,
Ripheus and Epytus, bravest in battle, revealed
    by the moonlight,
Join me as trusty friends, while Hypanis also, and
    Dymas   340

Take their place by my side, together with youth-
    ful Corœbus,
Offspring of Mygdon, who then, as it happened,
    had come to the city
Kindled at heart by a foolish and passionate love
    of Cassandra,
Bringing, for love to the daughter, his aid to the
    king and the Trojans;
Happier far had he heeded the counsel his bride
    in her frenzy   345
Uttered in vain.
When I perceive them close banded together and
    nerved for the conflict,
Thus I begin: 'Young men, brave hearts; alas,
    vain are the bravest!
If you still have the desire to follow me while I
    adventure
Certain destruction; for ours, as you see, is a
    desperate mission,   350
All of the gods in whose strength this empire was
    strong have deserted,
Leaving their altars and shrines; you run to the
    aid of a burning
Town; let us die; let us rush with all haste to the
    thick of the combat;
'T is the one safety of them that are conquered to
    hope for no safety!'
Thus, in the hearts of the youths desperation is
    kindled; thenceforward,   355
Like unto ravening wolves in the vapors of night,
    driven onward
Blind and mad with the torture of hunger, whose
    cubs, long deserted,
Wait them with parching throats, we go, through
    weapons, through foemen,

Marching to certain death, straight on through
    the heart of the city
Holding our course ; dark night hovers round us
    with shadowy pinions.   360
Who can untangle with words that night of death
    and of carnage ?
Who is able with tears to equal the flood of our
    sorrows ?
Crumbles the ancient town, after so many years of
    dominion.
Everywhere through the streets is a swath of mo-
    tionless bodies ;
Nay, through our very homes, and the hallowed
    halls of our temples.   365
Nor is the vengeance of blood from Teucrians only
    demanded ;
Sometimes courage returns even into the hearts of
    the vanquished ;
Some of our conquerors fall, there is ev'rywhere
    pitiful wailing,
Ev'rywhere trembling, and ev'rywhere Death's
    ever-multiplied image.
    First of the Grecians to meet us, Androgeos,
    heading his column,   370
Welcomes us gladly, believing that we are a
    friendly detachment,
Little he knows ! and offers us freely this kind
    admonition :
' Hasten, my men !   What slothfulness brings
    you so tardily hither ?
Here are the rest of us plundering Troy, and sack-
    ing the blazing
Citadel ; while ye now first come from the tower-
    ing vessels.'   375

Spoken had he, and, at once, for hardly assuring
    responses
Greeted his words, he perceived that he stood sur-
    rounded by foemen.
He was astounded, recoiling a step with an outcry
    of terror;
Just as a man who in struggling along amid briery
    brambles
Unexpectedly steps on a serpent, and, suddenly
    startled,   380
Shrinks as it rises in wrath, distending its collar of
    azure;
Not unlike him, did Androgeos tremblingly start
    when he saw us.
On them we rush, and encompass them round with
    the surge of our weapons,
Dropping them right and left, for terror had taken
    them captive,
Ignorant of the ground.   We are launched with a
    breeze of good fortune.   385
Flushed by victory, then, and exulting in spirit,
    Corœbus
Cries, ' O my comrades, where, first, kind fortune
    discloses a pathway
Leading to safety, and where she is beckoning,
    there let us follow !
Let us exchange our shields; on ourselves fit the
    Grecian devices;
Courage or craft in an enemy, who can be quib-
    bling about them ?   390
They shall themselves provide armor.' So say-
    ing, he puts on the crested
Helm that Androgeos wore, and his shield with its
    beautiful emblem,

While he adjusts to his side a sword of Grecian
    designing.
Ripheus follows his lead, and Dymas, and all of
    the others,
Youthful and glad, each arming himself from the
    newly won trophies.   395
On we advance, intermingled with Greeks, out of
    favor with Heaven,
And, in the blindness of night, as we run upon
    many a battle,
Join in the fight, and despatch not a few of the
    Grecians to Hades.
Others disperse to their ships, and hasten in flight
    to the faithful
Shores of the sea; and some, in ignominious ter-
    ror,   400
Climb back into the horse, and are hid in its well-
    known recesses.
    Ah! when the gods are offended, there's nothing
      't is right to confide in.
For, from the temple and shrine of Minerva a
    maiden is ravished,
Even the daughter of Priam, Cassandra, her hair
    in disorder,
Lifting her glittering eyes to Heaven in vain sup-
    plication,   405
Lifting her eyes, for her delicate hands are cruelly
    shackled.
This is a sight not brooked by the fiery soul of
    Corœbus;
Instantly, heedless of death, he springs to the
    midst of the rabble;
All of us follow his lead, and charge with our
    spears in a column.

Then we are first overwhelmed by a javelin-show'r
 which the Trojans   410
Hurl from the roof of a temple; then follows
 most piteous carnage,
Due to the style of our arms, the mistake of our
 Danaan helmets.
Then do the Greeks with a roar, enraged by the
 loss of the maiden,
Gather from every side, and attack us;—most
 furious Ajax,
Twins of Atreus, both, and all the Dolopian
 army;   415
Just as a bursting tornado, when winds from
 opposite quarters
Fiercely contend; both Zephyrus, Notus, and
 Eurus enjoying
Orient steeds; while forests are screaming, and
 foam-covered Neptune
Ruthlessly plunges his trident and churns the
 deep sea to the bottom.
Also, if any by guile in the darkness of night
 through the shadows   420
We have dispersed in flight, and scattered all over
 the city,
They, too, appear and, first, our shields and coun-
 terfeit weapons
Recognize, afterward noting the dissonant tones
 of our voices.
We are outnumbered and crushed in a moment,
 and first falls Corœbus,
Slain by Peneleus' hand at the shrine of the Goddess of Battle.   425
Ripheus also falls, and he was by far the most
 righteous

Ever was known in Troy, and the most observant
    of justice;
Otherwise thought the gods; both Dymas and
    Hypanis perish,
Pierced by their friends, nor, alas! did all thy
    devotion, O Panthus,
Shield thee when thou didst fall, nor the sacred
    bands of Apollo.   430
Witness, ye ashes of Troy, ye funeral fires of my
    people,
Witness that in your fall I shrank from no Da-
    naan weapons,
Shunned no hazard of Greeks; and, were it my
    fate to have fallen,
I had deserved it by valor. From thence we are
    suddenly hurried,
Iphitus, Pelias, I; but Iphitus already stag-
    gered   435
Under his years, while Pelias lagged with a wound
    from Ulysses.
Summoned by outcries, we hasten at once to the
    palace of Priam.
Here do we witness a battle indeed, as great as if
    nowhere
Other battles had been, nor any lay dead in the
    city;
Such is the fury of Mars, and the Greeks, how
    they charge on the palace!   440
See how the doorway is blocked; how the shields
    made a roof for the soldiers.
Ladders are hugging the walls; nay, right by the
    side of the doorposts,
Crowding the steps, with the left hand opposing
    their shields to the javelins,

Soldiers reach up with the right, and grapple the
    edge of the cornice.
Trojans, on their part, are tearing the tiles from
    the top of the palace,   445
Turret and roof, foreseeing the end, and prepare
    with such missiles
Means of defense in their struggle with Death,
    already triumphant ;
Also the gilded beams, their ancestors' proud deco-
    rations,
Tumble they down, while the rest draw sword and
    block every passage
Down below, where they stand on guard in a ser-
    ried battalion.   450
Kindled anew are our souls to relieve the imperial
    mansion,
Succor the men by our aid, and strengthen the
    hearts of the vanquished.
There was an entrance with secret doors, once
    used as a passage,
Joining the wings of the palace ; its entrance, a
    postern, neglected,
Gave on the rear ; by this, as long as the empire
    continued,   455
Hapless Andromache often had gone, unattended,
    to visit
Hector's parents, and little Astyanax lead to his
    grandsire.
Slipping in there, I mount to the topmost roof,
    whence the Trojans,
Pitiful sight, still hurled with their hands ineffec-
    tual weapons.
Right on the edge of the roof of the palace a tur-
    ret was standing,   460

Towering under the stars; all Troy and the Grecian encampments
Used to be seen from thence, and the Danaan
 ships in the harbor.
This we attack with our spears at a place where
 the uppermost stories
Loosening joints present; and, tearing it loose
 from its lofty
Seat, we topple it down; and, suddenly sliding, it
 tumbles   465
Wrecked, with a crash, and far and wide on the
 ranks of the Grecians
Falls; but others come up; and meanwhile, with
 no interruption,
Stones are filling the air, and missiles of every
 fashion.
Close to the entrance court, at the very doors of the
 palace,
Pyrrhus, exulting stands in a brazen glitter of
 armor,   470
Just as a snake that has fed on poisonous herbs,
 after lying
Swollen under the earth through the cold and the
 darkness of winter,
Now, renewing its youth, new clad in glittering
 splendor,
Rolls its slippery back in a coil, while its neck is
 uplifted
Into the light, and its three-forked tongue is in-
 cessantly flashing.   475
Next him is Periphas huge, and Automedon bearing his armor.
Armor-bearer now, once charioteer of Achilles.
All the Scyrian youth hurl brands to the roof of
 the palace.

Pyrrhus, himself, at their head, having seized a
    huge axe, double-bladed,
Breaks through the stubborn sills, and tears the
    bronze posts from their sockets :   480
Now he has cut out the beam, and hewn through
    the tough oaken timber.
What a wide gap he has made! what a yawning
    and terrible window
Showing the home within! long hallways open
    their vistas ;
Priam's apartments appear ; and the chambers of
    earlier monarchs ;
While, close up to the door, behold armed soldiery
    standing.   485
    Ah! but the home within, with wailing and piti-
    ful tumult
Grows confused, and, far in the inner court of the
    palace,
Hear that shrieking of women! The golden
    planets are startled !
Then through the spacious hallways, wander the
    shuddering matrons ;
Lo, they cling to the doors ; they are printing the
    portals with kisses.   490
On presses Pyrrhus, true son of his father, no
    bars can withstand him,
Nay, nor the guards themselves ; the door to his
    thunder incessant
Yields ; and the doorposts, hurled from their
    sockets, are falling before him.
Forcing their way, they burst in the doors, and the
    in-thronging Grecians
Butcher the first that oppose, and flood the broad
    hallway with soldiers ;   495

Not so madly the white foaming river sweeps over
    the cornfield,
Bursting its banks, and whirling away the dykes
    that oppose it,
Rolling its watery mass, and over the low-lying
    meadow,
Sweeping both herds and barns. I saw them in
    murderous frenzy,
Saw them myself in the doorway, Pyrrhus and
    both the Atridæ;   500
Hecuba, too, I beheld, and her hundred daughters,
    and Priam,
Quenching with bloody defilement the fires he had
    kindled to Vesta.
Those fifty chambers of marriage, strong hope of
    unbroken succession,
Fitted with doors of barbaric gold, and resplen-
    dent with trophies,
Sink to the dust, and the Greeks' hold fast where
    the flames are relenting.   505
  But, perchance thou are querying what were the
    fortunes of Priam.
When he hath witnessed the fall of the captured
    town, and the palace
Doors from their hinges torn, and the foe in the
    midst of his household,
Armor long disused, on shoulders aged and trem-
    bling,
Vainly the old man girds, and is belted about with
    his useless   510
Sword, and, resolved on death, runs to meet the
    dense throng of assailants.
Out in the court of the palace, and under the
    dome of the heavens,

There was an altar huge, o'erhung by a patriarch
    laurel,
Leaning over the shrine and folding the gods in
    its shadow.
Hecuba here, and her daughters, were crouching
    in vain by the altar, 515
Huddling like terrified doves in the gathering
    gloom of a tempest;
Clinging with desperate arms to the gods that
    were imaged in marble.
But, as her eyes beheld Priam, in youthful armor
    accoutred,
' Ah! my poor husband,' she cried, ' what purpose
    so frightful hath urged thee
Thus to be girded with arms? or where art thou
    rushing so madly ? 520
Not such assistance as thine, nor such defenders
    as thou art,
Times like these demand ; nay, not if my Hector
    were with us !
Yield to my prayer and come; we shall all be
    saved by this altar,
Or thou wilt die with us here.' Thus speaking,
    she tenderly drew him
Close to her side, and shielded his age in the sa-
    cred asylum. 525
But, from the slaughter of Pyrrhus escaped, lo,
    here is Polites,
One of the sons of Priam; he flies through the
    darts of the Grecians,
Down the corridors long, and dashes through
    courts all deserted,
Wounded ; while Pyrrhus, on fire, pursues him
    with threatening weapon ;

Now, even now, with his hand he hath touched him;
    now pressed with his spear-point.   530
Breaking away at last, right under the eyes of his
    parents,
Fainting he falls, and with torrents of blood is
    yielding his spirit.
Hereupon, Priam, though death already is closing
    about him,
None the less draws not back, nor checking his
    voice and his anger,
' Ay, may the gods,' he cries, ' if there be any jus-
    tice in Heaven   535
Heedful of such concerns, for a crime like this,
    for this outrage,
Render thee fitting thanks, and grant thee a just
    compensation,
Merited richly by thee who hast murdered my son
    in my presence,
Causing the blood of a son to defile the face of his
    father :
Nay, not Achilles himself, whom, thou liar, thou
    callest thy father,   540
He was not such toward Priam, his foe ; he blushed
    at dishonor,
Blushed at a suppliant's faith, and he gave the
    dead body of Hector
Back to the tomb, and me he returned unharmed
    to my kingdom.'
So spake the aged king ; and a spear ineffective,
    unwarlike,
Hurled ; but the ringing brass checked quickly
    the impotent weapon   545
Harmlessly hanging there in the outermost boss
    of the buckler.

Pyrrhus replied : ' Then take this message and go
    as informer
Unto my father Achilles, to whom of my infamous
    conduct
Fail not to speak, and remember your tale of de-
    generate Pyrrhus ;
Now dost thou die ! ' and, with this, he hath
    dragged him close to the altar   550
Trembling, and slipping about in the streaming
    blood of Polites.
Now with his left hand twined in his hair, his right
    draws a gleaming
Blade ; and now in his side to the hilt he hath
    buried a dagger.
This was the end to which Priam was destined ;
    this death was his portion ;
Fated to witness the burning of Troy, and the
    citadel falling ;   555
Yesterday, haughty king of so many countries and
    peoples,
Monarch of Asia ! he lies on the shore but a torso
    colossal,
Head from the shoulders torn, a nameless, un-
    recognized body.
  Then first, I myself, by cruel fear was encom-
    passed ;
I was dismayed ; there arose the form of my father
    beloved   560
As I beheld the king, of like age, with injuries
    mortal
Breathing away his life ; I thought of deserted
    Creusa,
Then, of my home, and then, of the peril of little
    Iulus.

Backward I look to discover what remnant of
    force is about me.

All have deserted, forespent; they have leaped
    from the roof in their terror,   565

Or to the flames in despair have given their suf-
    fering bodies.

Thus am I left alone; when down in the temple
    of Vesta,

Watching the door, and still, and shrinking back
    in the shadow,

Helen of Greece I see, bright flames giving light
    as I wander

Hither and thither, and turn my eyes on every
    object.   570

She, fore-dreading the Trojans enraged by the
    fall of their city,

Dreading the vengeance of Greece, and the wrath
    of her husband forsaken,

Common scourge that she was both of Troy and
    the land of her fathers;

There she hath hidden herself, and, detested, is
    crouched by the altar.

Burns in my spirit a fire; I dream in my rage of
    avenging   575

Teucria as she falls, of requiting the infamous
    traitor.

Shall she, indeed, with impunity, Sparta and na-
    tive Mycenæ

Greet with her eyes? Shall she go as a queen
    who has conquered, in triumph?

Husband, and parents, and children, and home, is
    she to behold them,

Tended by ladies of Troy, and served by Phrygian
    captives?   580

This, and Priam slain, and Troy still smoking in
    ashes ?
This, while all our coast still reeks with the blood
    of the Trojans ?
Never ! for, though it be true that vengeance
    wreaked on a woman
Wins no glorious name, though that victory bring
    me no honor,
Yet, to have ended the wretch, to have evened the
    balance of justice,   585
This will win ample praise ; and my soul shall
    exult in avenging
Fire, and rejoice to have paid a just debt to my
    countrymen's ashes.
While I was pondering thus, and yielding to furi-
    ous anger,
Lo ! there appeared by my side the benignant
    form of my mother,
Never so clearly revealed ; she gleamed through
    the night in her glory,   590
Owning her nature divine, and retaining the grace
    and the stature
Seen by the heavenly host, and, grasping my hand,
    she detained me,
While, with her roseate lips, she uttered a stern
    admonition :
' Son, what grief so profound hath aroused thine
    intractable anger ?
Why dost thou rage ? or whither hath vanished
    thy care for thy parents ?   595
First look where thou hast left thy father, aged
    and helpless ;
Where is Anchises now ?   Is thy wife Creusa still
    living ?

Little Ascanius, too?   All around them are bands
    of the Grecians
Roaming on every side, and now, but for my in-
    tervention,
Flames would have swept them away, and the
    sword of the enemy slain them.   ₆₀₀
Not the detested form of Laconian Tyndarus'
    daughter,
Nor the transgression of Paris; the wrath of Im-
    mortals, Immortals,
Now overthrowing thy realm, hurls Troy from the
    height of her glory.
Look! for the curtaining cloud that, veiling thee
    now as thou gazest,
Darkens thy mortal view and diffuses its vapors
    around thee,   605
I will wholly withdraw; nor of any behest of thy
    mother
Be thou afraid, my son, nor refuse to obey her
    commandments.
Here, where thou seest stone broken from stone,
    huge masses of ruin,
Columns of smoke and dust confusedly mingled
    together,
Neptune is heaving the walls by the might of his
    terrible trident,   610
Shaking their rock-bound beds, and wrecking the
    very foundations
Under the town; and here at the front, lo! piti-
    less Juno
Watches the Scæan gate, and summons her bands
    from the galleys,
Frenzied and girt with steel.
Now, on the roof of the castle, behold! Tritonian
    Pallas,   615

Gleaming in cloud and glittering shield, hath
    taken her station ;

Nay, the Great Father, himself, fresh courage and
    strength is imparting

Unto the Greeks; against Troy all the fury of
    heaven arousing.

ᵢFly, while thou canst, my son, and put an end to
    the struggle ;

I will not leave thee until thou art safely at home
    with thy father.'   620

Speaking no more, she was veiled by the deepening
    shadows of midnight.

Terrible forms appeared, and, arrayed against
    Troy, the embattled

Majesty of the skies.

Then, all Ilium seemed to me to be sinking in
    ashes,

Utterly overthrown the imperial city of Nep-
    tune ;   625

Yea, like an ancient ash that, crowning the crest
    of a mountain,

Peasants are struggling together to drag to the
    earth, after hacking

Round it with steel and with many an axe. It
    constantly threatens,

Bows its shuddering head of leaves, and, jarred to
    the summit,

Little by little now yields to its wounds, then utters
    a dying   630

Groan, and, torn from the hills, down crashes,
    majestic in ruin.

Now I descend, through flame and through foe,
    led on by the goddess,

Making my way, while weapons give place, and the
    fire shrinks before me.

Now, when at last I stood at the door of the home
    of my fathers ; —
Dear old home that it was ! — my father whom I
    was so anxious   635
First to bear to the hills ; yes, he whom first I was
    seeking,
Stoutly refused to prolong his life and suffer in
    exile
After the ruin of Troy ; ' O ye whose young
    blood is still coursing
Fresh in your veins,' he cries, ' whose strength
    still abides in its vigor,
Take ye thought for flight !   640
But, if the gods above had wished me to live any
    longer,
They would have spared my home. 'T is enough,
    and too much ! we have witnessed
One desolation, and once have survived the loss of
    our city.
Thus, O thus, as it lies, speak the last farewell to
    my body ;
Death with my hand I will find of myself, or the foe
    will have pity,   645
Seeking the garments I leave ; and a tomb, well,
    what does it matter !
Hated long by the gods, through profitless years
    have I lingered,
Since the Creator of gods and Ruler of mortals in
    anger
Touched me with finger of fire, and blasted my life
    with his thunder.'
Such were the words he repeated persistently, fixed
    in his purpose.   650
Meanwhile, bathed in tears, myself and Creusa
    together,

Little Ascanius, yea, the whole household, en-
    treated my father

Not to destroy us all, nor add a fresh pang to our
    sorrow.

Still he refused, still held unchanged his purpose
    and posture,

Driving me back to the fight, for death was the
    choice of my anguish.   655

What availed prudence now, what hope had for-
    tune to offer ?

That I could lift a foot, my father, if thou wert
    forsaken,

Hast thou believed ; or named with thy lips a
    crime so abhorrent ?

If the immortals have willed that so mighty a city
    shall perish,

If this be fixed in thy mind, and thou longest to
    add to the ruin   660

Both thyself and thine own, the door to that death
    is wide open ;

Pyrrhus will soon be here, still red with the mur-
    der of Priam ;

Son in the sight of the father, and father at altar
    he butchers.

Is it for this thou hast brought me, dear mother,
    through weapons and burnings,

Only to see the foe in the midst of my home, and
    to witness   665

Father, and son, and wife, Ascanius close to Creusa,

Huddled together in death, each stained by the
    blood of the other ?

Arms ! my men, bring arms ! the last morning is
    calling the vanquished.

Take me back to the Greeks ; rekindle the smoul-
    dering battle !

We may all die to-day, but not without tasting of
    vengeance !'   670
Then, again girded with steel, my left hand to the
    shield I was fitting,
While I was rapidly hastening out through the
    door of the palace.
Lo, however, my wife, embracing my feet on the
    threshold,
Clung to me there, holding out to his father our
    little Iulus.
'If thou art rushing to death, take us with thee
    wherever thou goest ;   675
But, if, through trial, thou hast any faith in the
    arms thou hast taken,
First defend this home. Who will care for our
    little Iulus ?
Who for thy father ? And whom has thy once
    honored wife to protect her ? '
    Shrieking these words aloud, she filled the whole
    house with her wailing,
When, unexpectedly, rises before us a marvelous
    omen   680
'Mid the embraces and parting words of his sor-
    rowing parents ;
For, a light tongue of fire appears on the head of
    Iulus,
Shedding a lambent light, and a flame, quite gentle
    and harmless,
Seems to be kissing his curly hair and caressing
    his temples.
Startled, and trembling with fear, we hasten to
    shake out the blazing   685
Hair, and strive to extinguish the sacred flame at
    the fountain.

Father Anchises, however, uplifting his eyes to
    the planets,
Joyously stretched his hands to the sky, and made
    his petition :
'Jupiter, lord of all, if prayers are ever availing,
Look thou upon us ; we ask no more ; and, if we
    are worthy,   690
Then, vouchsafe thine aid, O Father, and second
    these omens ! '
Scarce had the old man spoken these words, when,
    suddenly pealing,
Thundered the left, and a star rushed down from
    the sky through the darkness,
Drawing a glittering train, and passing in terrible
    splendor.
Then, after gliding high over the roof of the pal-
    ace, we saw it   695
Bury itself, unquenched, in the depths of the for-
    est of Ida,
Ploughing a flaming way, and then the long track
    of its furrow
Blazes with light, and widely around smokes the
    mountain with sulphur.
Then, indeed, overcome, my father slowly arises,
Speaks to the gods in prayer, and blesses the star
    they have sent him.   700
'Now, no longer delay ! wherever thou leadest, I
    follow.
Gods of my fathers, protect my home, watch over
    my children !
Yours is the augury ; Troy is still in your merci-
    ful keeping.
Yes, I yield, and now, my son, lead on and I fol-
    low.'

Yet, as he speaks, even now, through the town the
    fire is more clearly   705
Heard, and the billows of flame are rolling nearer
    and nearer.
' Come then, father belovéd, behold, my neck is
    thy refuge !
See ! my shoulders I bend ; such freight is no wea-
    risome burden.
Be the event as it may, our share of the danger is
    equal ;
Equal our share of hope; now, closely let little
    Iulus   710
Cling to my side, and my wife at a distance shall
    follow our footsteps.
You, my servants, to what I shall say, give closest
    attention :
There is a hill as you pass from the town, and a
    temple of Ceres,
Old and disused ; and a tree, an old cypress, is
    standing beside it,
Saved through all these years by the reverent faith
    of the fathers :   715
Following different paths, we shall meet in this
    common asylum.
Father, thy hand must receive our sacred utensils
    and hearth-gods ;
I, coming forth from so mighty a war, still reek-
    ing with slaughter,
Dare not approach them now ; nor until in a free-
    flowing fountain
I shall have bathed.'   720
Having thus spoken, my bended neck and the
    breadth of my shoulders
Covering with a cloak and the tawny skin of a lion,

Under my burden I rise ; to my right hand little
    Iulus
Tightly is clinging, and striving in vain to keep
    step with his father ;
Follows my wife behind, and we hasten along
    through the shadows.   725
Me, whom, an hour before, no rain of weapons had
    daunted,
No, nor the Greeks, though they charged in a mass
    from the front of the column,
Now each breeze dismayed, each sound now filled
    with disquiet,
Hesitant, doubly afraid for the charge of my hand
    and my shoulders.
And we were now drawing nigh to the gate ; we
    had turned the last corner,   730
Breathing more freely, when, all on a sudden, the
    trampling of footsteps
Rang in our ears, and then, peering forth through
    the shadow, my father
Shouted, ' Beware, my son ! away, my son ! they
    are coming !
Blazing shields and glittering brass, I see right
    before us.'
In my alarm, I know not what malevolent spirit 735
Seized my disordered mind, for, hurrying on
    through a by-path,
When I had passed from the beaten track of the
    well-known highway,
Woe is me ! my wife, Creusa, was torn from my
    bosom
By some grievous fate ; did she stop ? did she
    stray ? was she weary ?
No one can tell ; but, alas, she was never restored
    to our vision ;   740

Nay, I looked not back to discover my loss, nor
    was troubled

Till we had come to the mound of ancient Ceres,
    and entered

Into her sacred shrine; but there, when we all met
    together,

One was not; one failed her friends and her son
    and her husband.

Whom of the gods or of men did I spare in my
    foolish upbraiding?   745

What more cruel thing had I seen in the desolate
    city?

Little Ascanius, father Anchises, the Trojan
    Penates,

All I entrust to my friends and hide in a shelter-
    ing hollow,

Then seek the city again, and am girded with glit-
    tering armor,

Bent on renewing all risks, resolved all Troy to
    retraverse,   750

Ready once more to hazard my life, to confront
    every peril.

    First, I retrace my way to the walls and the
    shadowy gateway

Whence I had made my escape; and, closely ob-
    serving my footsteps,

Follow them back through the night and trace them
    by flashes of firelight.

Horror is all around, the very silence affrights
    me.   755

Thence I haste to my home, if perhaps, — if per-
    haps, — she has thither

Guided her feet. The Greeks have rushed in and
    are crowding our dwelling;

All is now lost; fierce flames are wreathing the
    roofs of the turrets,
Surges of fire arise, and roll to the heavens in
    fury.
Yet I go on to the palace of Priam and visit the
    castle;   760
Already now in the desolate courts, in Juno's
    asylum,
Guardians chosen for might, both Phenix and sav-
    age Ulysses,
Keep their eyes on the spoil; for hither the Teu-
    crian treasures
Snatched from blazing shrines are brought from
    all parts of the city;
Sacred tables, and stolen robes, and bowls from
    the temple,   765
All of pure gold. An array of boys and shud-
    dering matrons
Hover around.
    Then I even dared to drive my voice through
    the shadows,
Filling the streets with my cries and sadly shout-
    ing ' Creusa,'
Vainly repeating her name, and calling it over and
    over.   770
Still I was searching and rushing distractedly over
    the city,
When the unhappy form, yea, the spirit itself, of
    Creusa,
Rose before my eyes, a familiar but glorified image.
Bristled my hair with fright, and my tongue be-
    came speechless with terror.
Then, unclosing her lips, she spoke and ended my
    trouble :   775

'Why doth it please thee, my husband belovéd,
    to yield to this frantic
Passion of grief? These events come not without
    sanction of Heaven.
Thou art forbidden to carry Creusa to share in
    thine exile!
This is forbidden by him, who is throned upon
    lofty Olympus.
Banishment long for thee! thou must plough the
    great plain of the ocean;   780
Yea, thou shalt come to that Western land, where
    Lydian Tiber
Rolleth his peaceful tide through fields that bring
    wealth to the people.
There prosperity waits, and a throne; and, a
    daughter of princes,
There is a wife for thee; weep not for thy cher-
    ished Creusa.
I shall not look on the Myrmidon homes, nor
    Dolopian grandeur,   785
Nor shall I go as a slave to serve the Pelasgian
    matrons;
I! a Dardanian princess, and child of the Queen
    of the Heavens;
But the Great Mother of gods detaineth me here
    in her mountains;
Now, farewell, and cherish thy love for the son I
    have borne thee.'
When she had spoken thus, she left me weeping
    and longing   790
So many things to say; like a mist of the morning
    she vanished.
Thrice I attempted to throw my arms round her
    neck as she stood there,

Thrice, unavailingly clasped, the vision denied my
    embraces
Like the light kiss of the wind, still more like a
    dream in its swiftness.
  So, at last, when the night is done, I return to
    my comrades;   795
Here, with amazement, I find a great number of
    faithful companions,
Comrades new who have gathered here, both ma-
    trons and heroes,
Youth, also, banded in exile, — a wretched and
    mournful assembly, —
Flocking from every side, and prepared with heart
    and with treasure
Bravely to follow my lead o'er the sea, not ques-
    tioning whither.   800
Now o'er the rugged brow of Mount Ida the day-
    star was rising,
Ushering in the dawn; and the Greeks were hold-
    ing the guarded
Entrance of every gate; Troy needed my succor
    no longer.
Yielding, at last, I caught up my father and fled
    to the mountain.

BOOK III

After it pleased the gods to destroy the Asian
    kingdom,
Even.the guiltless nation of Priam; when Ilium,
    haughty,   `
Fell, and all Neptunian Troy lay smoking in
    ashes,
We, by tokens divine, are driven abroad into
    exile,
Seeking an unknown land; and under the walls of
    Antandros,   5
Under the Phrygian mountain of Ida, we fashion
    our galleys,
Knowing not whither the Fates may lead, where
    grant us a refuge.
Likewise we gather our men. It was only the
    dawning of summer
When ' Give sails to the Fates ' was the order of
    father Anchises.
Then I abandon with tears my native shorè, and
    the harbor,   10
Yea, and the plain where Troy hath been. I am
    borne as an exile
Over the deep, with my son and my friends, my
    gods and Penates.
    There is a distant land, broad-fielded, well-peo-
    pled, and warlike,
Tilled by the Thracians, and formerly governed by
    daring Lycurgus,

Ancient confederate friend of Troy, in a holy
 alliance,   15
Long as our star shone bright. Hither-borne, I
 erect on its winding
Shore my earliest walls, — for the Fates were already against me, —
Making a name from my own, and calling my
 people Æneads.
Down on the shore, I was offering gifts unto Venus,
 my mother,
And to the gods who preside over new undertak-
 ings ; a shining   20
Bull was I slaying for Jove, great king of the
 dwellers in heaven.
Near me, by chance, rose a mound whose top bore
 bushes of cornel,
Also the lance-like wands of a bristling thicket of
 myrtle ;
This I approached, but, when I endeavored to
 pluck the green branches
Up from the earth, that with dark leafy boughs I
 might cover the altars,   25
Dreadful and strange to relate was the omen that
 greeted my vision ;
For, as with snapping roots the bush first torn
 from the hillock
Yields to my hand, dark drops of blood ooze out,
 and with crimson
Color the earth. Cold chills unnerve my shiver-
 ing body,
While my freezing blood congeals with shuddering terror.   30
Still do I venture once more to gather another
 tough cornel,

Seeking deeply to probe the mysterious cause of
    the portent ;
When, from the bark of the second, lo ! drops of
    dark blood again trickle.
Anxiously pondering then, I entreated the nymphs
    of the woodland,
Father Gradivus, too, for he cares for the fields of
    the Thracians,   35
That they would hallow the sight, and graciously
    lighten the omen.
But, as again and with greater force I pull at the
    saplings,
Struggling hard with my knees on the sand that
    resists my endeavor,
Shall I be silent or speak ? There arises the
    mournfullest moaning
Out of the depths of the earth, and a voice replies
    as I listen :   40
' Why dost thou mangle my body, Æneas ? Why
    trouble my slumber ?
Spare me ! Spare to defile thine innocent hands.
    Not an alien
Unto thyself was I born in Troy ; and not from a
    cornel
Trickles this blood. Ah ! fly from this covetous
    shore, from this cruel
Land ! Polydorus am I, and here transfixed, hath
    an iron   45
Harvest of spears overwhelmed me, and grown to
    a forest of lances.'
Verily then by a twofold fear was I troubled in
    spirit ;
Bristled my hair with fright, and my tongue be-
    came speechless with terror.

Long before this, when first he despaired of the
    arms of the Trojans,
Seeing the city already surrounded and closely
    beleaguered,   50
Sorrowful Priam had secretly sent to the king of
    the Thracians
This Polydorus, with treasure of gold, to be reared
    in the palace;
He, when the power of the Trojans was broken,
    when Fortune had left them,
Joining the side of the Greeks, and choosing vic-
    torious standards,
Violates every right; Polydorus he murders, and
    seizes   55
Forcibly on the gold.   Accurséd hunger for
    riches,
Unto what crime constrainest thou not the spirit
    of mortals!
After my terror subsides, I report to the chiefs of
    my people,
First to my father, the signs of the gods, and beg
    for their counsel.
All are agreed in mind; to depart from the infa-
    mous country,   60
Flee from the treacherous land, and give the
    south winds to our galleys.
Therefore we pay Polydorus the honors of burial,
    raising
High o'er his grave a mound, and an altar we
    build to his spirit,
Mournful with fillets of black, and dark with fu-
    nereal cypress.
Matrons of Troy attend, with hair unbound, as our
    way is;   65

Then, after this, new milk in foaming vessels we
    offer,
Chalices also of sacred blood, giving rest to his
    spirit
There in the grave, and, at last, with loud fare-
    wells do we leave him.
Then, when first we cau trust to the deep, and the
    winds give a quiet
Sea, and the southern breeze, low whispering, calls
    to the ocean,   70
Then my companions uncable their ships, and
    throng to the beaches.
Outward borne from the harbor, the cities and
    shores are retreating.
There's a delightful land in the midst of the sea.
    It is sacred
Both to the Nereids' mother, and Neptune who
    rules the Ægean;
Once it went drifting from shore to shore, but holy
    Apollo   75
Linked it securely to Myconos, moored it to Gya-
    ros lofty,
Rendered it safe to be lived in, and taught it to
    laugh at the tempests.
Hither I drift; this island of peace, with its shel-
    tering harbor,
Welcomes the weary; we land, and worship the
    home of Apollo.
Anius, king of the people, and priest of the Tem-
    ple of Phœbus,   80
Fillets and sacred wreaths of laurel encircling his
    temples,
Hastens to greet us, and finds an old friend in my
    father Anchises.

Then do we join right hands in friendship, and en-
    ·ter their dwellings.
  I was adoring the god in an ancient temple of
    marble : —
'Grant us, O Phœbus, a home of our own ; grant
    walls to the wearied ;   85
Children vouchsafe, and a permanent town ; pro-
    tect the new city ;
Save us, a remnant escaped from the Greeks and
    from cruel Achilles.
Whom shall we follow ? Or where dost thou bid
    us to go ; where to settle ?
Grant us, O Father, a sign ; yea, make of our
    spirits thy temple.'
Scarcely had this been said, when ev'rything sud-
    denly trembled,   90
Lintel, and laurel divine ; the whole mountain
    about us was shaken,
And, as the doors of the shrine were unfolded,
    loud rumbled the caldron.
Humbly we fall to the earth ; the oracle speaks,
    and we listen :
'Brave-hearted Trojans, the land that at first
    from the stock of your fathers
Fostered your earliest growth, the same shall re-
    ceive you with gladness,   95
Safe to her bosom restored ; ye must patiently
    seek your old mother.
There shall the sons of Æneas be masters of every
    sea-coast,
They and their children's children, and all genera-
    tions that follow.'
Phœbus hath uttered these words : then rise loud
    shouts of rejoicing ;

While we all question what land this may be;
    and whither Apollo,   100
Ordering us to return, is calling the wanderers
    homeward.
Then, my dear father, recalling the legends of
    primitive heroes,
Cries, ' Give ear, O chiefs, and learn of the hopes
    you inherit;
Crete, an island of Jove supreme, lies far in the
    ocean;
There is Mount Ida, and there is the cradle that
    cherished our nation;   105
Populous cities an hundred are there, most fruitful
    dominions;
Thence, if I rightly recall the tradition, the first
    of our fathers,
Teucer, was carried, in days of old, to the Rhœ-
    tian sea-board;
There chose a place for his realm. Not yet was
    Ilium standing,
Nor the proud castles of Troy; the people dwelt
    low in the valleys;   110
Hence the Great Mother of Cybela, hence Cory-
    bantian cymbals,
Hence the Idean grove, and the rites of mysteri-
    ous silence,
Also the lions in harness that bow to the yoke of
    their mistress.
Come then, and whither the gods have shown us
    the way, let us follow.
Let us invoke the winds; let us haste to the Gno-
    sian kingdoms;   115
Not far distant are they; let Jupiter only be with us,
And the third morning shall anchor our fleet in the
    port of the Cretans.'

Thus having spoken, he slew at the altar appro-
    priate victims ;
Offered to Neptune a bull, and a bull unto thee,
    bright Apollo ;
Black was the lamb for the Storm, and white for
    the favoring Zephyrs.   120
  Flies a report that Idomeneus, forced to surren-
    der his sceptre,
Hath from the realm of his father withdrawn, that
    the shores are abandoned,
Houses free from a foe, and dwellings deserted
    and empty.
Leaving Ortygia's harbor, we spread our sails to
    the ocean ;
Coasting the Bacchanal mountains of Naxos, and
    verdant Donysa,   125
Skirting Olearos, Paros, pure white, and the Cy-
    clades scattered
Over the sea; through straits that are fretted by
    clustering islands.
Shouts of the sailors arise with varied and glad
    emulation,
Calling aloud to each other, ' Sing ho ! for Crete
    and our fathers ! '
Rising astern, a breeze follows after us hastening
    onward,   130
Till we glide at last to the ancient coast of the
    Cretans.
Eagerly then do I build the walls of my long
    wished for city,
Calling it Pergamum, urging the citizens, proud of
    their title,
Ever to love their homes, and to guard them by
    building a fortress.

High and dry had most of our galleys been drawn
    on the seashore;   135
Occupied were our youth with weddings and work
    in the cornfields;
I was ordaining laws and homes; when a wasting
    infection
Suddenly fell on our frames from a tainted tract
    of the heavens;
Over our trees and crops came a piteous blight,
    and a season
Fruitful in death; men died, or dragged about
    suffering bodies;   140
Sirius parched our fields, and left them barren and
    wasted;
Scorched was the grass, and the withering corn
    portended a famine.
Back to the shrine of Ortygia, back to Apollo, my
    father
Urged us to go, to retraverse the sea, and to pray
    for his mercy;
Asking what end he will give to our trouble, and
    whence he will have us   145
Seek relief from our woes, or whither continue
    our journey.
  Now it was night, sleep holding the earth and
    the souls of the living,
When the sacred forms of the Phrygian gods
    and Penates
Which I had brought from Troy, from the midst
    of the flames of the city,
Seemed to be standing before my eyes in a dream
    as I slumbered.   150
Clearly they stood revealed, and were crowned
    with a halo of glory

Where the full moon was pouring her light
    through the deep sunken windows.
Then, addressing me thus, they spake and relieved
    my foreboding :
' What Apollo would say if Ortygia thou shouldst
    revisit,
Here he reveals of his own accord, sending us to
    thy threshold.   155
We who, since Troy was burned, have accom-
    panied thee and thy fortunes,
We who have measured with thee the heaving
    main in thy galleys,
We, yes we, will exalt to the stars thy future de-
    scendants ;
We will secure to thy city dominion.   'T is thine
    to establish
Bulwarks of might for the mighty.   Fear not the
    long labor of exile ;   160
Thou must remove thy home ; these shores are not
    for thy dwelling ;
Thou art not bidden to settle in Crete by Delian
    Apollo ;
There is a place which is known as Hesperia, —
    named by the Grecians, —
Ancient the land, prevailing in arms and abound-
    ing in harvests,
Settled at first by Œnotrian men ; it is said their
    descendants   165
Now have entitled the race from the name of their
    leader, Italian.
This is our proper abode ; our Dardanus sprang
    from this country
(Father Iasius, too) the prince who founded our
    nation.

Come, then, arise! and report to thine aged father
    with gladness

These undeniable words: it is Corythus he is to
    search for,   170

And the Ausonian land; Jove denies thee the
    meadows of Dicte.'

Stunned by a vision like this, by the voice of my
    hearth-gods astounded,

(Nor was that sleep profound, but I seemed to re-
    cognize plainly

Features and fillet-bound locks, and to see their
    faces about me;

Then, too, an icy sweat was starting all over my
    body,)   175

Springing up from my couch, I stretch to the hea-
    vens my open

Palms, and cry aloud, and sprinkle a holy libation

Over the hearth; and then, having finished the
    sacrifice, gladly

Hasten Anchises to tell, and unfold the whole
    story in order.

Frankly he owns our double descent, our claim to
    two founders;   180

Also his error through modern confusion of an-
    cient tradition,

Then he exclaims, 'Dear son, sore chastened by
    Ilium's downfall,

None but Cassandra predicted to me so grievous
    disaster;

Now I remember she chanted that this was the
    fate of our nation;

Often she sang of Hesperia, often of Italy's em-
    pire;   185

But who could ever believe that unto Hesperian
    harbors

Trojans would come! or whom could Cassandra
    convince by her visions?
Let us to Phœbus yield; we are warned, let us
    follow more wisely.'
Thus does he speak, and we all acquiesce in his
    words with rejoicing.
This home, too, we abandon, and leaving a few of
    our comrades,   190
Spreading the sails of our hollow barks, we skim
    the wide ocean.
  After our boats had gained the deep, and land is
    no longer
Now to be seen, but on all sides the sky, and on
    all sides the water,
Then, right over my head, there lowers a leaden-
    hued storm-cloud,
Bringing night and a storm, and shudder the waves
    in the darkness.   195
Presently winds are rolling the sea, great billows
    are rising,
Scattered are we o'er the vast abyss, and tossed by
    the surges;
Clouds have enshrouded the day, rain and dark-
    ness have hidden the heavens;
Lightnings redouble their strokes from the clouds
    that are riven asunder;
Wildly we drive from our course, and drift o'er
    the dark heaving waters.   200
Palinurus, himself, declares that he cannot distin-
    guish
Night from day in the sky, nor remember his way
    in the ocean.
Thus, for three uncertain days, we grope in the
    darkness

Blindly over the sea; three starless nights do we
    wander.

When the fourth day was come, land seemed at
    last to be rising,   205

Mountains loomed up in the distance, and volumes
    of smoke were discovered.

Sails drop down; we rise on our oars; no delay,
    but the sailors

Bend to their toil, and scatter the foam, and sweep
    the blue water.

Saved from the waves, the shores of the Stropha-
    des first give me refuge,

Strophades, called by a Grecian name; they are
    islands uplifted   210

Out of the great Ionian sea, where dreadful Ce-
    læno

Dwells with her sisters dire, from the time they
    abandoned in terror

Banquets they used to share, till barred from the
    Phinean palace.

Monster more fell than they, nor any more utterly
    cruel

Curse and scourge of the gods, e'er rose from the
    Stygian waters.   215

Vultures envisaged like virgins, polluted below and
    polluting,

Such are the Harpies, with claws for hands, and
    their faces with hunger

Pallid for aye.

When, hither-drifted, we enter the harbor, behold,
    all about us

Herds of cattle are seen contentedly grazing the
    lowlands;   220

Also a flock of goats, untended, are cropping the
    herbage.

On them we rush with our darts, and invoke to
    their share of the booty
Jove, himself, and the gods, and then, on the curve
    of the seashore,
Build our couches high and prepare for a gener-
    ous banquet.
But, with a frightful swoop, the Harpies come
    down from the mountains,   225
Taking us unaware, then, screaming and flapping
    their pinions,
Tear at our meat, and defile the feast by their
    odious contact,
Uttering fearful cries, and emitting a pestilent
    odor.
Then, in the depths of a cave, in the sheltered re-
    treat of a cavern,
Hedged all about by trees, and darkened by bris-
    tling shadows,   230
Spread we our tables again, and rekindle the fire
    on our altar ;
But from the opposite sky, and down from dark
    places of hiding,
Circling their prey again, with crooked talons, the
    noisy
Flock come flying, and foul the feast by their
    beaks.   Then I order
Arms to be seized by my friends ; and war to be
    waged on the monsters.   235
Strictly obeying my words, they bury their swords
    in the grasses,
Hidden from sight, and conceal their shields, and
    wait for the combat.
So, when the noise of their swooping resounds on
    the wide-curving beaches,

Loud from his lofty watch Misenus trumpets the
    signal;

Then my comrades attack, and attempt a new
    fashion of battle,   240

Trying to maim with their swords these flying
    pests of the ocean;

But no weapon can pierce their skin, or injure
    their plumage;

Swiftly they fly away, and soar aloft in the hea-
    vens,

Leaving their half-eaten prey and the loathsome
    marks of their talons.

One of them perches aloft on a cliff of the moun-
    tain, Celæno,   245

Prophetess of despair, and thus gives vent to her
    curses:

' Sons of Laomedon, offer ye war for the death of
    our bullocks?

Or for our heifers slain? or are ye prepared for
    the battle

Thinking to drive from their native realm the in-
    nocent Harpies?

Take, then, these words of mine to your hearts,
    and never forget them,   250

Words which to Phœbus the Father Supreme, and
    which Phœbus Apollo

Hath unto me foretold. now I, who am Queen of
    the Furies,

Utter. For Italy now are ye bound, and, appeas-
    ing the tempests,

Italy shall ye gain, and be suffered to enter her
    harbors;

But no walls shall arise around that city of
    promise   255

Till, constrained by dire distress, for the crime of
    our slaughter,
Ye shall have hungrily gnawed with your teeth,
    and eaten your trenchers.'
Speaking, she rose on her wings, and disappeared
    in the forest;
But, with a sudden chill of dread, the blood of my
    comrades
Froze in their veins; their hearts were afraid, and
    no longer with weapons,   260
Rather with vows and prayers, for peace they were
    fain to petition,
Whether to spirits divine or to vultures fierce and
    ill-omened.
Father Anchises, too, uplifting his hands on the
    seashore,
Called on the mighty gods, ordaining due sacrifice
    for them.
'Silence these threats, ye gods! Ye gods, avert
    such disaster;   265
Graciously keep thy servants in peace.' Then he
    ordered the cable
Torn from the shore, and the ropes to be shaken
    out ready for action.
South winds fill the sails; we flee o'er the white
    foaming breakers
Whither our course and the wind and the pilot are
    bidding us follow.
Now there appear in the midst of the sea the
    groves of Zacynthos;   270
Later, Dulichium, Samos, and Neritos lofty and
    rock-bound;
Swiftly we flee by the Ithacan crags, and the realm
    of Laertes,

Cursing the land that had cradled the childhood
    of cruel Ulysses.

Soon, too, the storm-crowned peaks of Leucata are
    looming before us ;

Rises also the fane of Apollo, the terror of
    sailors.   275

This we weariedly seek, and steer to the quaint
    little city ;

Anchors are dropped from our bows, and the shore
    is fringed with our galleys.

• Thus, in spite of our fears, at last we are come
    to a haven,

And, with purified hands, we worship at Jupiter's
    altar,

Honoring also the Actian shores with Ilian con-
    tests.   280

Stripped, and supple with oil, my comrades prac-
    tise the wrestling

Learned in their native land ; well pleased to have
    safely avoided

So many Grecian towns, to have slipped through
    the midst of their foemen.

Meanwhile, the sun sweeps around the majestic
    path of his orbit,

And, with his northern blasts, chill winter roughens
    the waters.   285

Then, to the front of the temple, the shield of
    proud Abas I fasten,

Hollow and forged of brass ; and add this metrical
    legend :

'This is the armor Æneas hath captured from
    conquering Grecians.'

Then I give orders to loose from the port ; 'To
    your oars, to your benches ! '

Eagerly striking the sea, my comrades are sweep-
    ing the billows.   290
Presently leaving behind us the airy summits of
    Corfou,
Coasting the shore of Epirus, we enter Chaonia's
    harbor
Safely, and come, at last, to the towering walls of
    Buthrotum.
Here our ears are surprised by an almost incredi-
    ble story;
Even that Helenus, Priam's own son, Greek cities
    was ruling;   295
Nay, had obtained the wife and the crown of
    Æacian Pyrrhus,
And that again to a husband of Troy had Andro-
    mache fallen.
I was amazed, and my heart was inspired with a
    wonderful longing
Unto the hero to speak, and learn the strange tale
    of his fortunes.
So I go up from the port, leaving shore and ves-
    sels behind me,   300
Just as by chance, near the gates of the city, An-
    dromache offered
Funeral gifts and a yearly feast in a grove by the
    feignéd
Waters of Simois unto the dead, and was mourn-
    fully calling
Hector's shade to the empty turf-covered tomb, and
    the altars
Twain she had hallowed there as a sacred asylum
    of sorrow.   305
Now, when she saw me draw near, and beheld with
    amazement the Trojan

Armor that compassed me round, appalled by the
    strange apparition,
Rigid, and fixedly staring, she stood ; life's heat
    left her body ;
Falling, long time she lay, unable to speak ; then
    she murmured,
' Art thou a living form ?   Dost thou verily bring
    me a message ?   310
Goddess-born, then dost thou live ? or, if life's
    kindly light hath departed,
Where is my Hector ? ' She spoke, and wept,
    and with loud lamentation
Filled the whole place ; I could say but a word
    now and then as she wildly
Raved, but in deep distress I faltered a few broken
    answers :
' Surely I live, and prolong my life amid infinite
    trouble ;   315
Doubt not the vision is true.
Ah, but what fate hath o'ertaken thee, robbed of
    so noble a husband ?
Or, what return of good fortune hath worthily
    raised thee to honor ?
Hector's Andromache, art thou consenting in mar-
    riage to Pyrrhus ? '
Dropping her eyes, with a tremulous voice she
    sadly responded :   320
' O, above all, how supremely blest was that
    daughter of Priam
Bidden to die at her enemy's tomb, under Troy's
    lofty ramparts !
Happy that maiden for whom no lots have been
    cast, and who never
Hath in captivity touched the bed of a conquering
    master !

We, when our city was burned, through sea after
    sea were transported,   325

We have endured the scorn of the haughty heir of
    Achilles, —

Mother and slave in one, — and then when he left
    me to follow

Leda's fair daughter, Hermione, — seeking alliance
    with Sparta, —

Me, as a slave to a slave, into Helenus' hands he
    delivered.

Then, Orestes, aflame with passionate love for his
    stolen   330

Bride, and urged by the Furies of Crime, surprised
    him, and slew him,

While he was off his guard, at the altar his fathers
    had builded.

When Neoptolemus died, a part of the realm he
    abandoned

Fell to Helenus' lot, who named the Chaonian
    lowlands, —

All Chaonia named, — from the name borne by
    Chaon, the Trojan ;   335

Pergamum, too, he hath built on the hills, and this
    Ilian fortress.

But, what winds have directed thy course ? what
    destiny guided ?

Or, to our shores what god hath driven thee on-
    ward so blindly ?

What of the boy, Ascanius ? Is he yet living and
    breathing ?

Whom unto thee in Troy —   340

Nay, but the boy, — is he grieving still for the loss
    of his mother ?

Or have his father Æneas and Hector, his uncle,
    bequeathed him

Something of ancient pride, and something of
    manly endurance ? '
Thus she continued with sobs, then burst into vio-
    lent weeping.
Useless, alas, are tears ! when down from the city
    the hero,   345
Priam's own Helenus came, attended by many
    companions ;
Recognized his friend, and led us with joy to his
    threshold,
Fain to shed tears himself in the midst of his
    greetings of welcome.
Then I go on, and a tiny Troy, and a citadel
    copied
After her mighty tower, I recognize, also a Xan-
    thus   350
Thirsty and small; and I gather a Scæan gate to
    my bosom.
All my Trojans, too, are welcomed as guests of the
    city ;
Unto his spacious abode the king in person invites
    them.
There, in the midst of the hall, they pour a liba-
    tion to Bacchus ;
Served is a banquet in gold, and their hands lay
    hold of the wine-cups.   355
  "Now, that day and the next have flown, and
    breezes arising
Call to our sails, and the wind of the South is
    swelling our canvas.
Then to the prophet I speak these words, and ask
    him these questions :
' Trojan-born, mouthpiece of God, who knowest
    the will of Apollo,

Thou who knowest the caldrons, the Clarian laurel,
    the planets,   360
Also the language of birds, and the portent of
    swift-flying pinions,
Tell me, I pray, for a kind revelation hath guided
    my journey
All the long way, and all of the gods by their
    omens have urged me
Italy to pursue, and her far distant shores to ad-
    venture;
Only the Harpy, Celæno, new horrors unlawful to
    utter   365
Prophesies, threat'ning the curse of her terrible
    anger and vengeance,
Even a famine malign; what perils must first be
    avoided?
Under whose lead can I finally conquer these fear-
    ful disasters?'
Hereupon, Helenus, first invoking the gods for
    their favor,
Sacrificed bullocks according to custom; then
    loosened the fillets   370
Binding his sacred brow, and me to thy portals,
    O Phœbus,
Led by his holy hand, overawed by thy manifest
    presence.
Then, with his lips divine, thus chanted the Priest
    of Apollo:
'Child of a goddess, — for sure is my faith that
    thy galleys are sailing
Under a prosperous star, for the King of the gods
    is directing   375
Destiny thus, thus shaping thy fortune; this course
    is determined; —

I will unfold to thy view a few of his manifold
 counsels ;
So shalt thou traverse more safely the prosperous
 sea, and find refuge
In the Ausonian port; but the rest Fate hides
 from thy knowledge,
Nor doth Saturnian Juno give Helenus leave to
 discover. ₃₈₀
Italy, first, that thou thinkest so near, already pre-
 paring
Neighboring harbors to enter, not knowing the
 truth, this is sundered
Far, by a path untried and long and by far-reach-
 ing countries ;
Also thine oars must first be bent in Trinacrian
 waters,
Thou must pass over the plain of Ausonian brine
 with thy vessels, ₃₈₅
And thou must visit the Lake of Shades and the
 Island of Circe,
Ere in a peaceful land thou canst hope to establish
 a city.
I will reveal the signs ; do thou hold them fixed in
 remembrance.
When by thine anxious eyes an enormous sow is
 discovered
Near to the bank of a darkling stream, under
 shore-shading oak-trees, ₃₉₀
When thou shalt see her outstretched on the
 earth, the mother of thirty
Young, and, white herself, giving breast to a white
 brood around her,
There shall thy city be set ; yea, there shalt thou
 rest from thy labors.

Tremble no more with dread of that threat of a
    " gnawing of trenchers,"
Fate will provide a way, and Apollo, invoked, will
    be with thee.   395
But, this country of ours, and the coast-line of
    Italy's sea-board
Nearest at hand, and washed by the tides that our
    sea is up-rolling,
This thou must shun, for its towns are all peopled
    by desperate Grecians.
Here, the Narycian Locrians dwell in a fortified
    city ;
Also the Sallentine plains hath Cretan Idomeneus
    crowded   400
Thick with his troops; and Philoctetes, here, a
    chief Melibœan,
Little Petelia rules, Petelia trusting in bulwarks.
Furthermore, when thy fleet, after coursing the
    sea, shall be anchored,
When thou shalt offer thy vows on the shore that
    shall welcome thine altars,
Muffle thy face, and cover thy head with a mantle
    of purple,   405
Lest some evil eye meet thine and trouble the
    omens,
While in the name of the gods the hallowed
    flames are arising.
Let thy companions continue this rite; do thou
    also retain it ;
Yea, let thy reverent children maintain this ob-
    servance forever.
But, when the wind shall have shifted thy course
    toward Sicily's headland,   410
When the close straits of Pelorus begin to grow
    wider before thee,

Then must thou turn to the land on thy left, and
    the sea to the southward,
Making a long detour; shun the shore and the
    waves to the northward.
Once these regions were rent by the throes of a
    mighty convulsion,
Such are the changes wrought by the endless suc-
    cession of ages,   415
Torn apart, it is said, though anciently one and
    unbroken
Both these shores; and the sea hath forced a rough
    passage between them,
Sundering Italy's flank from Sicily; pouring its
    narrow
Tide between cities and fields, once joined, now
    rudely dissevered.
Scylla is guarding the shore on the right, and
    hungry Charybdis   420
Watches the left, and thrice each day in the depths
    of her yawning
Cavern she gulps far down in her throat the pre-
    cipitous waters,
Belching them forth in turn, and drenching the
    sky and the planets.
Scylla, however, lurks hidden from sight in cav-
    erns of darkness,
Reaching out with her jaws, and shattering ships
    on her ledges.   425
Human her form above, a maiden of beautiful
    bosom
Down to the waist; but, below, an enormous and
    hideous monster,
Dolphin-like tails conjoined to a girdle of ravening
    sea-wolves.

Better it were to delay, and round the Trinacrian
    headlands,
Doubling Pachynus and making a long and weari-
    some circuit,   430
Rather than once to have looked upon Scylla far
    off in her monstrous
Cave, and the rocks that resound with the howls
    of her brine-colored sea-dogs!
Further, if Helenus hath any wisdom, if in his
    foreknowledge
Any reliance be placed; if Apollo hath truly in-
    spired him,
One thing there is, O child of a goddess, one more
    than all others,   435
I will foretell and forewarn thee, repeating it over
    and over.
First, invoke with prayer the presence of powerful
    Juno;
Chant unto Juno thy willing vows, and with sup-
    pliant off'rings
Conquer the mighty queen; for so, from Trinacria
    parting,
Thou shalt be guided at last in triumph to Italy's
    borders.   440
When thou art thither borne, drawing nigh to the
    city of Cumæ,
Nearing the lake divine, and Avernus rustling with
    forests;
There, in a cave of the rock, shalt thou find a mad
    writer of verses
Chanting the fates, and committing to leaves her
    letters and phrases.
All the prophetic songs she hath written on leaves
    doth the virgin   445

Lay in an orderly row, and leave in her cavern
    secluded.
Motionless there they remain in their places, nor
    stir from their order;
Nevertheless, when the hinges are turned, and a
    breeze hath disturbed them,
When the light breath of the door the delicate
    leaves hath disordered,
Never again doth she care, as they flutter about in
    the cavern,   450
Either to catch and arrange them aright, or re-
    couple her verses.
Wise as you came you depart, reviling the home
    of the Sibyl.
Here, let no cost of delay appear in thine eyes of
    such moment,
Though thy companions be ne'er so impatient,
    though urgent thy voyage
Call to the deep thy sails, though favoring gales
    be inviting,   455
But that thou visit the Sibyl and beg her to chant
    her predictions
Then and there; till her voice and her lips be
    unsealed in thy favor.
She will advise thee of Italy's people, of wars that
    await thee,
Also how best to avoid or endure each coming dis-
    aster,
And in response to thy prayer will grant thee a
    prosperous voyage.   460
This is all of thy future my lips are permitted to
    utter.
On, then! and by thy deeds exalt great Troy to
    the heavens.'

After these words with his friendly lips the pro-
    phet had spoken,

Gifts that were heavy with gold, and ivory carv-
    ings, he ordered

Carried down to the ships; and stowed a ballast of
    silver   465

Over their curving keels; gave also Dodonæan
    caldrons,

Adding a corselet of gold with triplicate links in-
    terwoven,

Also the cone and the flowing crest of a marvel-
    lous helmet,

Armor of Pyrrhus; and then, there were personal
    gifts for my father;

Horses he added, and guides;   470

Fitted our galleys with oars, and provided my
    comrades with weapons.

  "Meanwhile Anchises commands to make ready
    the sails for the galleys

So that no time may be lost when the wind shall
    invite our departure.

Him, then, the priest of Apollo addresses with
    courtly politeness:

'Thou who art proudly and worthily wedded to
    Venus, Anchises,   475

Care of the gods, twice rescued by them from a
    city in ruins,

Yonder, behold thine Ausonian land! Sail forth
    and possess it!

Nevertheless, thou must pass beyond this land on
    the ocean;

Far is that part of Ausonia destined for thee by
    Apollo.

Onward, then, blessed by the love of thy son! What
    need of prolonging   480

Speech? Or wherefore delay the rising wind by
    discourses?'

Then, Andromache, too, no less grieved at our
    parting forever,

Brings to Ascanius garments embroidered in fig-
    ures, with threadwork

Woven in gold; and a Phrygian cloak, and, with
    unsurpassed bounty,

Loads him with gifts of her loom, and says, as she
    presses them on him,   485

'Take these, also, dear boy; of my hands may
    they ever remind thee;

Long may they speak to thee, too, of the love of
    Andromache, Hector's

Wife; receive them, then, as the farewell gifts of
    thy kindred;

Thou, the one copy I have of my little Astyanax'
    image!

Thine are the eyes, and the hands, and thine are
    the lips of my darling;   490

Just of thine age, he, too, would now be attaining
    to manhood.'

Tears then filled my eyes, and I said, while turn-
    ing to leave them,

'Farewell, happy pair, whose lot is already deter-
    mined;

Summoned are we to pass from one strange fate
    to another,

Ye have attained your rest; by you no field of the
    ocean   495

Waits to be ploughed; nor must Italy's plains, for-
    ever receding,

Still be pursued; ye look on the pattern of Troy,
    and a Xanthus

Which your own hands have made, and I hope
    with far happier omens;
Destined I trust to be free from Grecian invasion
    forever.
If I shall ever have entered the Tiber and gained
    the fair meadows   500
Fringing its bank, and have seen a city vouchsafed
    to my people,
Then, our cities fraternal, our nations united by
    kinship,
Yours in Epirus, in Italy ours, both having one
    founder,
Dardanus; having, moreover, a common fate, we
    will make them
Both one Troy in heart; let this be the care of our
    children.'   505
  " Over the sea we are borne, close by the Cerau-
    nian mountains,
Whence is the shortest way to Italy over the wa-
    ter.
Meanwhile the sun rushes on, and the mountains
    are darkened in shadow.
Then we are stretched on the breast of the coveted
    land, by the seaside.
Watchers we draft for the oars, and, scattered
    along the dry beaches,   510
Strengthen our hearts with food, and refresh our
    tired bodies with slumber.
Not as yet have the Hours borne Night through
    half of her circuit,
When Palinurus, alert, springs up from his couch
    and examines
All of the winds, and listens attent to the voice of
    the breezes;

Notices all the stars as they glide through the si-
    lence of heaven,   515
Studies the Hyades stormy, and studies the Bears
    and Arcturus;
Carefully studies the golden belt and the sword of
    Orion.
Seeing that all is at peace in the cloudless heavens,
    a cheerful
Signal he gives from the deck; we move our en-
    campment, and venture
Forth on our way, outspreading the wings of our
    sails to the night-wind.   520
Now had the stars been driven to flight, and Au-
    rora was blushing,
When, far away, we behold dark hills; land
    stretching below them.
'Italy! Italy!' first Achates cries with rejoicing;
'Italy!' all my companions salute with glad ac-
    clamation.
Then doth my father Anchises enwreathe a huge
    bowl with a garland;   525
Now he hath filled it with wine, and now on the
    gods he is calling,
Standing aloft on the stern:
'Gods of the sea and shore, ye gods who govern
    the tempest,
Hasten our prosperous way by your winds; breathe
    graciously on us.'
Freshens the coveted breeze, and opens before us
    the harbor,   530
Distant no longer; and crowning the height is a
    fane of Minerva.
Then do my friends furl sail, and turn our prows
    to the mainland.

Curved by the eastern wave to the form of a bow is
 the harbor ;
Foaming with briny spray are the cliffs confronting the ocean ;
Hidden the port, for the towering crags, with a
 double escarpment,   535
Lower their mighty arms, and the temple retreats
 from the shore-line.
Here my first omen I see ; four horses abroad in
 the meadow
Browsing the plain at large ; four horses shining
 and snow-white.
Father Anchises cries : ' Strange land, thou be-
 tokenest battle,
Horses are ready for battle ; of battle these herds
 are a menace.   540
Yet to the wain these very steeds once used to be
 subject,
Bowing their necks to the yoke, and peacefully
 wearing a harness ;
Still there is hope of peace.' Thereupon we in-
 voke the fair goddess,
Pallas, resounding in arms, who hath welcomed us
 first in our gladness,
Veiling our heads at her shrine with mantle of
 Phrygian purple ;   545
Also, obeying the precepts which Helenus urgently
 gave us,
Duly we offer the honors commanded to Juno of
 Argos.
Tarrying not, as soon as our vows have been duly
 accomplished,
Round to the sea we turn the horns of our sail-
 covered yard-arms,

Leaving the homes of the children of Greece, and
  the fields we distrusted.   550
Next, on the bay of Tarentum, a city, if rumor be
  trusted,
Founded by Hercules, rises, across from Lacinia's
  temple ;
Also Caulonia's tow'rs, and that wrecker of ships,
  Scylacæum ;
Then, afar off, looms up from the surge Trinacrian
  Ætna ;
Also we hear the deep groan of the sea, rocks
  beaten by breakers   555
Far in the distance ; and then, the sullen roar of
  the beaches ;
Leap the deep waters of ocean, and sand and wave
  are commingled.
Father Anchises, then : ' This, truly, is frightful
  Charybdis ;
These are the cliffs and the terrible rocks of which
  Helenus warned us.
Save us, my men ! arise ! arise on your oars ! all
  together ! '   560
All they are bidden, they do ; and first Palinurus
  has sharply
Whirled to the left the prow till it roars in the
  rush of the water;
Then the whole fleet bears hard to the left with
  oar and with canvas.
Up we are raised to the sky, as the sea arches
  under our galleys,
Then, as the wave gives way, we sink into regions
  infernal ;   565
Thrice in caverns of stone is a roaring of rock all
  around us ;

Thrice have we seen the foam dashed up, and the
  firmament dripping.
Meanwhile the wind goes down with the sun,
  deserting us wearied.
Ignorant, then, of our way, we drift to the shore
  of the Cyclops.
  " Safe from the entrance of winds is the har-
    bor itself, and capacious;   570
But, on one side, with most terrible noises, Mount
  Ætna is roaring;
Sometimes hurling aloft in the sky black clouds,
  and a murky
Whirlwind of smoke, whose gloom is filled with
  glimmering cinders,
Shooting up balls of fire that glitter high in the
  heavens;
Sometimes, belching, it raises rocks, and tearing
  the entrails   575
Out of the mountain, whirls the molten mass to
  the zenith,
Roaring aloud and boiling up from its very foun-
  dations.
There 's a tradition that under this mountain En-
  celadus' body,
Half consumed by the lightning, is crushed, while
  ponderous Ætna,
Over him hurled, breathes flame from furnaces
  bursting asunder;   580
Also, as oft as he shifts his wearied side, with a
  murmur
All Trinacria trembles, and smokes till the heavens are darkened.
All that night in the sheltering wood we endured
  the terrific

Omens, unable to see what it was that occasioned
    the uproar;
For there was neither the light of stars, nor a
    firmament shining   585
Bright in a peaceful sky, but clouds in a heaven
    of darkness,
While the untimely night imprisoned the moon in
    a storm-cloud.
    Now in the farthest East, the morning already
        was breaking,
Yea, Aurora had swept from the sky the shadowy
    vapor,
When from the wood, on a sudden, emerges the
    form of a stranger,   590
Clad in pitiful rags, a wasted, emaciate figure.
Then, as entreating our aid, he stretches his hands
    to the seashore.
Backward we turned; there was dreadful filth;
    his beard was neglected;
Thorns held his clothing together; the rest beto-
    kened a Grecian;
One who of yore had been sent to Troy with the
    ships of his nation.   595
As for himself, when he saw from afar our Dar-
    danian garments,
Saw the armor of Troy, he was frightened, and
    faltered a moment,
Checking his steps; but, soon, he swiftly rushed
    down to the seashore,
Throwing himself on our mercy with tears: ' By
    the stars, by the Powers,
Yea, by the light of the sky, by this air that we
    breathe, I conjure you,   600
Spare me, O men of Troy! To what country
    soever ye take me

That will suffice ; it is true that I have embarked
    with the Grecians ;
Yea, I confess that your Ilian homes I have rav-
    aged in battle ;
If, on this account, the guilt of my crime be so
    grievous,
Scatter me over the wave, or drown me deep in
    the ocean ;   605
If I must die, I shall gladly have died by hands
    that are human.'
Having said this, he embraced our knees ; to our
    knees in his writhing
Still did he cling. We exhort him to tell what
    family claims him ;
Then to explain what fate is the cause of his great
    agitation.
Father Anchises, himself, gives the youth his right
    hand in a moment,   610
Reassuring his mind by a pledge so cordially
    offered.
Finally, laying his fear aside, he tells us his story :
' Ithacan born am I, a friend of unhappy Ulysses.
I, Achemenides, went to Troy, Adamastus, my fa-
    ther,
Being so poor ; ah, me ! to be back in those days
    of my childhood !   615
Here, in the depths of the cavern of Cyclops, my
    comrades forgetful
Left me behind as they fled from his cruel abode
    in their terror.
It is a house of blood ; of blood are the feasts it
    hath witnessed ;
Dark within, and huge ; its master so tall that his
    forehead

Strikes the high stars; ye gods, remove from the
    earth such a monster!   .   620
One who devours the flesh, and drinks the dark
    blood of his victims,
Looked on by none without fear, and spoken to
    never by any.
I have seen him myself, when flat on his back in
    his cavern,
Two of our number, gripped in his giant hand, he
    was dashing
Dead on the rock, while the floor ran red with the
    blood that was scattered.   625
When he was crunching their bodies, from which
    black gore was exuding,
While the limbs, yet warm, quivered under his
    teeth, I beheld him;
Not unpunished, indeed; such things were not
    brooked by Ulysses,
Nor in a crisis so great was the Ithacan shorn of
    his cunning;
For, when gorged with the horrible feast and
    stupid with drinking   630
He had reclined his drooping neck, and stretched
    through the cavern
All his enormous bulk, while he vomited blood in
    his slumber,
Blood and morsels of flesh with bloody wine inter-
    mingled,
We, having prayed to the gods, drew lots, and
    gathered about him;
Then his eye, that enormous eye that used to lie
    sunken,   635
Sunken and single beneath his terrible brow, like
    a Grecian

Shield, or the lamp of Apollo, we bored with a
    well-sharpened weapon,
Yea, at last we rejoiced to avenge the shades of
    our comrades.
But, O wretched men, flee away, flee away, and
    your cables
Burst from the shore !   640
For, as grim and as huge as Polyphemus who
    gathers
Wool-bearing ewes in his hollow cave, and presses
    their udders,
There are an hundred more dread Cyclops who
    thickly inhabit
All these curving shores, and roam these towering
    mountains.
Now are the horns of the moon for the third time
    filling with brightness,   645
While I am dragging out life in the woods 'mid
    the haunts and deserted
Lairs of ferocious beasts, peering forth from the
    rock of the giant
Cyclops, and trembling with fear at their tread
    and the sound of their voices.
Boughs have yielded my meagre fare, hard cornels
    and berries,
And with their uptorn roots the herbs of the field
    have sustained me.   650
Sweeping all with my eyes, this fleet of yours I
    discovered
First approaching the shore, and to this, whatever
    might happen,
Trusted my life. 'T is enough from that cursed
    tribe to be rescued ;
Take ye my life away, by whatever death; it were
    better.'

"Scarce had he spoken thus, when behold, on
    the crest of the mountain,   ₆₅₅

Moving amid his flocks, with body enormous, the
    shepherd,

Polyphemus himself, coming down to his haunts
    by the seashore!

Monster terrific, deformed, gigantic, and robbed
    of his vision.

Grasping the trunk of a pine, he guides and
    steadies his footsteps;

Wool-bearing sheep are about him, and they are
    his only enjoyment,   ₆₆₀

Only solace of ill.

Soon as the crested wave he hath touched, by the
    shore of the ocean,

Then, from his hollowed eye he washes the blood
    as it trickles,

Gnashing his teeth with a groan; and, now,
    through the sea is he striding,

Nor as yet have his lofty flanks been wet by the
    breakers.   ₆₆₅

Then far away with a shudder we hasten our flight,
    taking with us

Him who had prayed so well; and we silently
    sever our cable;

Then, with emulous oars, bend forward and sweep
    o'er the water.

This he perceives, and turns his step to the sound
    of our voices.

But as soon as he finds that his hand is unable to
    seize us,   ₆₇₀

When he no longer can breast the Ionian tides in
    pursuing,

Then he utters a roar so loud that the sea and the
    surges

Tremble together with fear, and Italy's heart is
    affrighted,
Yea, even Ætna reëchoes the roar in her deep
    winding caverns.
But, from the woods and the lofty hills, the tribe
    of the Cyclops,   675
Startled, rush down to the harbor and crowd the
    shore of the ocean ;
Brethren of Ætna, we see them all standing in im-
    potent fury,
Each with his frightful eye, uplifting his head to
    the heavens ;
Horrid assembly, they ! As when, on the top of
    a mountain,
Towering oak-trees stand, or cone-bearing cypresses
    cluster,   680
Forming a lofty forest of Jove, or a grove of
    Diana.
Urgent fear with headlong haste constrains us to
    loosen
Halyards at random, and stretch our sails to the
    care of the breezes ;
Yet the injunctions of Helenus warning us not to
    go forward
'Twixt Charybdis and Scylla — two paths with
    little distinction   685
Leading to death ; — we determine to turn our
    sails to the southward.
Lo ! however, sent forth from the narrow straits
    of Pelorus,
Boreas comes : I am borne by Pantagia's mouths
    in the living
Rock, past Megara's bay, and the low-lying city
    of Thapsus.

Such were the shores, as we carried him back o'er
    the course he had traversed,   690
Achemenides showed us, the comrade of wretched
    Ulysses.
  Stretching before the Sicilian bay lies an island
    confronting
Foaming Plemyrium, once Ortygia called by the
    ancients.
There is a story that hither Alphēus, a river of
    Elis,
Burrowed his lonely way through the sea. He
    now, Arethusa,   695
Through thy fountain commingles his tide with
    Trinacrian waters.
Heeding command, we adore the powerful gods of
    the country.
Thence I pass the too fertile soil of stagnant He-
    lorus,
Next, the lofty cliffs and jutting rocks of Pachy-
    num
Coast we along; and, afar, Camarina appears,
    whose removal   700
Even the Fates forbade; and the lowlands of Gela,
    and Gela
Taking its name from the name of the mighty and
    turbulent river.
Lofty Acragas, then, uplifts her proud walls in the
    distance,
Acragas, formerly known as the breeder of spir-
    ited horses.
Thee, too, palmy Selinus, I leave, by the winds
    that are granted;   705
Coasting along thy reefs and dangerous shoals,
    Lilybæum;

Next, the harbor and joyless coast of Drepanum
    greet me.
Here, after beating my way through so many
    storms of the ocean,
Here, alas, did I lose my father Anchises; my
    greatest
Comfort in care and grief; it was here, O noblest
    of fathers,   710
Thou didst forsake me, outworn, thou, rescued in
    vain from such perils.
Helenus, wise as he was, when he warned me of
    manifold horrors,
Never foretold this sorrow to me ; nor did fright-
    ful Celæno.
This was the final blow; this the goal of my pil-
    grimage weary.
When I departed thence, heaven drove me down
    to your seacoast."   715
Thus was Father Æneas, alone, while all were
    attentive,
Telling the fates of the gods, and rehearsing his
    wandering courses.
He became silent at last, and, ending the story, he
    rested.

BOOK IV

Ah, but the queen, long since sore hurt by the
    arrows of Cupid,
Feeds her love with her life, and is secretly wasted
    by passion.
Constantly runs in her mind the man's great worth,
    and the noble
Honor that crowns his liue; his words and his
    looks are still clinging
Fixed in her heart, and love disquiets the peace of
    her slumber.   5
So, when Aurora next lighted the earth with the
    torch of Apollo,
When she had swept from the sky cool night with
    its mist-laden shadows,
Thus, all distracted, she cried to the answering
    heart of her sister,
" Anna, dear sister, what dreams are affrighting
    me, sad and bewildered !
What strange guest is this who hath entered our
    home !   How distinguished   10
Both in his face and mien !   And his heart, how
    brave, how heroic !
I, for one, and with reason, believe him descended
    from Heaven.
Fear betrays low-born souls ; but, alas, by what
    cruel misfortune
He hath been ever pursued !   What wearisome
    wars he recounted !

Dwelt there not in my heart a fixed and immova-
 ble purpose 15
Never again to consent to be linked to another in
 wedlock,
Since my first love failed, since Death deceived
 and bereft me,
Were I not utterly weaned from the torch and the
 chamber of marriage,
Unto this one reproach I might, perhaps, have
 surrendered.
For, I will own, dear Anna, that since the sad fate
 of Sichæus, 20
Since by my brother's crime our home was defiled
 and dishonored,
This man alone hath stirred my heart, and mastered my spirit.
Yielding, I feel once more the glow of long slumbering passion.
But I had rather the earth should yawn to its
 depths underneath me,
Rather the Father omnipotent strike me down
 with his thunder 25
Where in profoundest night pale shades of Erebus
 wander,
Rather, my honor, than violate thee, or break thy
 requirements.
He who wedded me first took with him my heart
 when he left me;
Still let him keep his own; in his tomb let him
 guard it forever."
Speaking these words, with a torrent of tears she
 deluged her bosom. 30
Anna replies, " O thou, who art dearer than life to
 thy sister,

Wilt thou in loneliness pine, till the days of thy
    youth are departed,

Knowing no children sweet, and enjoying no bless-
    ings of Venus?

Thinkest thou ashes will care; or the shades of the
    buried be troubled?

Grant that no lover before hath won thy heart
    from its grieving,   35

Either iu Libya now, or aforetime in Tyre; bid
    Iarbas

Go, if thou wilt, with scorn, and the rest of the
    African princes,

Mighty in war; yet, why resist a love that delights
    thee?

Hath it not crossed thy mind whose lands these are
    thou hast settled?

Here are Gætulian towns, a race unconquered in
    battle, —   40

There wild riding Numidians press, and impassa-
    ble quicksands.

Here is a region made desert by drought, and rav-
    aged by roaming

Barcans; and why do I speak of Tyre and its
    omiuous war cloud,

Or of our brother's threats?

Guided by Heaven, I believe, and under the favor
    of Juno,   45

Hither these Ilian keels have found their way in
    the tempest.

What a proud city, my sister, thou yet shalt
    behold! What a nation

Spring from a match like this! With the arms
    of the Trojans to help us,

By what illustrious deeds shall we heighten the
    glory of Carthage!

Seek but the favor of Heaven, and when thou hast
    gained absolution,   50
Then be as kind as thou wilt ; find reasons to keep
    him delaying
Long as the seas are rough, while stormy Orion is
    raging ;
Urge his shattered ships, and plead the implacable
    heavens."
Thus by her words she fanned the flame that pas-
    sion had kindled,
Thus freed a wavering heart from the bondage of
    fear and of honor.   55
   First they visit the temples, and pass from altar
    to altar,
Paying their vows ; and sheep, selected according
    to custom,
Offer to law-giving Ceres, to Phœbus, and father
    Lyæus,
But, before all, unto Juno, the guardian goddess
    of marriage.
Holding the cup in her own right hand, most
    beautiful Dido   60
Empties it fairly between the horns of a snow-
    white heifer ;
Or, invoking the gods, draws nigh to the rich laden
    altars,
Hourly renewing her gifts, and still, as each sheep
    is laid open,
Watches with lips apart, and questions the quiver-
    ing vitals.
Ah ! unseeing seers ! What balm can your vows
    and your temples   65
Bring to a wounded heart ? For still the soft
    flame without ceasing

Feeds on her life; and the hidden wound still
    lives in her bosom.
Dido, on fire with love, goes wandering on through
    the city,
Frantic and sore distressed, like a deer that a
    shepherd pursuing,
Drawing his bow at a venture, hath pierced afar
    off and unwary,   70
Deep in the Cretan groves, and, unwitting, aban-
    dons his arrow;
But, as the wounded deer goes roaming the forests
    of Dicte,
Still in her side as she flies, the fatal arrow is
    clinging.
Now she guides Æneas along through the midst
    of the city,
Shows him the wealth of Tyre, and her capital
    nearly completed;   75
Opens her lips to speak, and stops with the sen-
    tence unfinished.
Then, as the day declines, she invites him again to
    a banquet,
Begs, in her frenzy, to hear once more the Trojan
    disasters,
Hangs for the second time on his lips as he tells
    her the story.
Then, when her guests are gone, and the moon in
    turn disappearing   80
Puts out her light, and the stars as they set are
    inviting to slumber,
Lone in her empty hall she is sad, and the couch
    he has quitted,
Presses, and, absent, sees and listens to him who
    is absent;

Or to her bosom she folds Ascanius, charmed by
  his father's
Likeness, if thus, perhaps, she may cheat her un-
  speakable longing.   85
Towers forget to rise ; armed youth no longer are
  marshalled
On the parade ; all work on harbor and walls is
  suspended ;
Buildings abruptly stop ; the threatening crest of
  the rampart
Stands unfinished and bare, and the towering der-
  ricks are idle.
  Soon as the consort belovéd of Jupiter sees her
    o'er-mastered   90
Thus by the fever of love, and modesty yielding to
  passion,
Quickly with words like these Saturnia turns upon
  Venus : —
" Truly, with honor unheard of, and glorious
  trophies thou comest,
Thou and this boy of thine !   Thy name shall be
  great and immortal !
If by the cunning of two of the gods one woman
  be vanquished,   95
Yet I am not so blind, for I know that thou fear-
  est our bulwarks,
Watching the rising homes of Carthage with se-
  cret misgiving.
Where shall we make an end ?   What profits a
  quarrel so bitter ?
Shall we not rather agree on perpetual peace, and
  a union
Sanctioned by both ?   Thou hast gained what thy
  heart hath been set on securing ;   100

Did , is burning with love; her heart is surging
    with passion;

Let us with equal authority govern a nation
    united;

Dido shall yield her hand to the hand of a Phry-
    gian husband,

She sh`ll entrust to thee her dowry of Tyrian sub-
    jects."

Then, (for she clearly perceived how craftily Juno
    had spoken,   105

Hoping that Italy's power might be turned to the
    African seacoast,)

Thus did Venus reply: "Is there any so mad as
    to question

Terms like these, or prefer to engage in a quarrel
    with Juno?

If we could only be certain that fortune would fa-
    vor the project.

But I have come to distrust the fates; whether
    Jupiter wishes   110

These who have come from Troy to unite with the
    people of Carthage,

Whether he favors this blending of blood, and
    these bonds of alliance;

Thou art his wife; 't is thy right to coax him to
    show thee his purpose.

Lead, I will follow." Then thus quick answered
    imperial Juno:

"Mine shall that duty be. And now, I will briefly
    advise thee   115

How what remains to be done can be done most
    successfully: listen!

Into the forest together Æneas and heart-stricken
    Dido

Plan to go hunting to-morrow as soon as the ʼrch
    of Apollo
Flashes above the sea, unveiling the earth with its
    glory.
Over them, then, the blackness of clouds, commin-
    gled with hailstones,   120
I will outpour from the sky, and shake the whole
    welkin with thunder
While their horsemen are spreading their toils and
    enclosing the jungles ;
Then shall their comrades be scattered and cov-
    ered by midnight darkness ;
Dido and Ilium's lord shall reach the same cavern,
    together ;
I will be there, and if thou wilt only vouchsafe us
    thy blessing,   125
I will proclaim the bans and join them by mar-
    riage forever ;
This their wedding shall be." Cytherea, by no
    means reluctant,
Nodded assent to the plan and laughed as the plot
    was unfolded.
    Meanwhile Aurora, arising, has left the waves of
    the ocean.
Chivalrous youth of Tyre ride out of the gates
    with the sunrise,   130
Laden with nets and toils, and hunting-spears
    bladed with iron.
Libya's knights rush forth with kennels of keen-
    scented boar-hounds.
Still, as the queen in her chamber delays, the
    princes of Carthage
Wait at her gates ; and, proud in his trappings of
    gold and of purple,

Stands her own hunter, impatiently champing his
    foam-covered snaffle.   135
Lo, she appears at last, encompassed by thronging
    attendants;
Woven with colors the border that fringes her
    Tyrian mantle;
Quiver of gold she bears, with gold she hath fas-
    tened her tresses;
Golden the girdle below, that binds her vesture of
    purple.
Also advancing come Trojan retainers, and joyful
    Iulus,   140
While Æneas, himself, surpassing all others in
    beauty,
Graces the sport with his presence, and mingles
    his train of attendants,
Like to Apollo, when, Lycian winter and hurrying
    Xanthus
Leaving behind, he visits the home of his mother
    in Delos.
There he renews the dance, and around bacchana-
    lian altars,   145
Cretans chant, and Dryopians dance with tattooed
    Agathyrsi;
But on the hilltops of Cynthus he walks, inter-
    twining his wind-tossed
Hair with a light pressing chaplet of gold and
    leaves of the laurel;
Arrows clang on his back. With no less grace
    doth Æneas
Move than he; while beauty as godlike shines in
    his features.   150
    Soon as the mountains were reached, and the
    trackless haunts of the jungle,

Wild goats leap from the ledges, and scamper
    with pattering hoof-beats
Over the hilltops, and columns of deer, in the op-
    posite quarter,
Thunder their way o'er the shelterless fields, until
    all the stampeding
Dust-covered ranks unite in flight, and abandon the
    mountains.   155
But, in the midst of the plain, Ascanius, boy-like,
    rejoices,
Proud of his horse; and, swiftly outrunning one
    after another,
Prays that instead of these spiritless herds a boar
    may be granted,
Or that his vows may bring from the mountains a
    tawny-skinned lion.
Meanwhile, the heavens are filled with an ominous
    rumble of thunder,   160
Followed at once by a storm of rain commingled
    with hailstones.
Hither and thither the Tyrian train and the Tro-
    jan retainers,
E'en the Dardanian grandson of Venus, have
    sought in their terror
Huts dispersed through the fields; wild torrents
    rush from the mountains.
Dido, the queen, and the Lord of Troy have
    reached the same cavern.   165
Then, first of all, Mother Earth and Juno, the
    goddess of wedlock,
Giving the signal, the lightnings blaze for torches
    of marriage,
Flames the conspiring sky, and nymphs loudly
    wail on the hilltop.

That day first foretokened her death and fore-
    shadowed her anguish,
For, no longer disturbed by visions of sin or of
    scandal,   170
Dido, contented no longer with loving her lover
    in secret,
Cloaks her disgrace with a name, and calls Æneas
    her husband.
    Instantly Rumor goes flying through all the great
    Libyan cities,
Rumor, a curse than whom no other is swifter of
    motion.
Ever on swiftness she thrives, and gains new vigor
    by speeding.   175
Cringing at first with fear, she lifts herself quick
    to the heavens,
Treading still on the earth, but veiling her face in
    the storm-cloud.
Earth brought her forth, it is said, impelled by
    her rage against heaven.
She was the latest born of the terrible sisters of
    Titan.
Swift are her feet, and swifter the flight of her
    hurrying pinions;   180
Monster terrific and huge, who, under each sepa-
    rate feather,
Carries a watchful eye; by each eye, O marvellous
    story!
Babble a tongue and a mouth, and an ear pricks
    forward to listen.
Rustling, she flies by night, between earth and sky
    in the darkness,
Never closing her eyes in the sweet refreshment of
    slumber;   185

Watching by day like a spy, she perches aloft on
    the housetops,
Or upon lofty towers, and causes great cities to
    tremble;
Tale-bearer, loving the truth no better than slan-
    der and libel.
Such was the one who was filling the nation with
    manifold rumors,
Gloating, and equally glad whether telling a truth
    or a falsehood.   190
How that Æneas had come, a descendant of an-
    cestors Trojan,
How that to him fair Dido had deigned to surren-
    der her honor,
How that in luxury now they were idling away
    the long winter,
Caring no more for their kingdoms, enslaved by
    an infamous passion.
Such were the stories the hideous goddess was
    scattering broadcast.   195
Suddenly then she veers in her course to the court
    of Iarbas,
Kindles his wrath by her words, and adds new
    flame to his fury.
He, the descendant of Ammon, who ravished the
    nymph Garamantis,
Temples an hundred to Jove in his wide-spreading
    realm had erected,
Altars an hundred had built, and vowed to keep
    burning upon them   200
Slumberless fires, for the gods a perpetual care;
    and a pavement
Rich with the blood of sheep, and gates ever
    blooming with garlands.

There, with frenzied heart, and maddened by tid-
    ings so bitter,
He, it is said, fell prone, in the presence divine, by
    the altar,
Urgently pleading with Jove, with hands out-
    stretched in petition: 205
" O thou omnipotent Jove, unto whom the Mauru-
    sian nation,
Feasting on couches of purple, now offer their
    sparkling libations,
Seest thou this ?   Or is it for naught that we
    tremble, O Father,
When thou art hurling thy bolts ?   And the flames
    in the clouds that appal us,
Are they but random fires, and vain, ineffectual
    rumblings ?   210
Here is a woman who, straying among us, on land
    that we sold her,
Founded a beggarly city; we gave her our shore-
    lands for tillage,
Granted her also the rights of the land ; now, hav-
    ing rejected
Marriage with us, she hath opened her realm to
    her lover, Æneas ;
Nay, at this moment, that Paris, subserved by
    effeminate courtiers,   215
Glistening locks and beard by a Phrygian bonnet
    enfolded,
Revels in stolen love ; while we, forsooth, to thy
    temples
Come to present our gifts, and cherish an empty
    tradition."
When he had uttered this prayer, and while he
    yet clung to the altar,

Jove, the omnipotent, heard, and directed his eyes
    to the royal   220
Town, and the lovers there, forgetful of nobler
    tradition.
Mercury then he addresses, and these are the man-
    dates he utters:
"Up and away, my son! call zephyrs, and haste
    on thy pinions,
And to this Dardan lord who yonder in Tyrian
    Carthage
Lingers, and cares no more for the cities the Fates
    have vouchsafed him,   225
Speak; yea, ride on the winds and deliver him
    these my commandments:
This is not what his most glorious mother hath
    prophesied of him,
Neither for this hath she rescued him twice from
    the sword of the Grecians;
But to be one who should govern an Italy pregnant
    with empires,
Sounding aloud with war; a man who should
    prove by his valor   230
Kinship with Teucer of old, and bow the whole
    world to his sceptre.
Yet, if no vision of glorious victory kindle his
    spirit,
Though, for his own renown, he covet not labor
    and hardship,
Yet, shall a father withhold the castles of Rome
    from Iulus?
What is his plan? By what hope is he held in
    the midst of his foemen?   235
Hath he forgot his Ausonian line, and Lavinian
    meadows?

Bid him, in short, set sail. Let this be the sum
    of our message."
Then to obey the commands his omnipotent father
    hath uttered,
Mercury hastens, and first to his ankles he fastens
    his wingéd
Sandals of gold, which bear him aloft with the
    speed of the whirlwind,   240
Whether above the land or over the plain of the
    ocean.
Then he assumes the rod which he bears when he
    summons from Orcus
Pallid shades, or remands the remainder to regions
    infernal.
Slumber he gives and takes, and he opens the eyes
    of the dying.
Trusting to this, he urges the winds and rides on
    the storm-clouds ;   245
Now he beholds in his flight the peak and high
    ridges of Atlas, —
Atlas the rugged, supporting the sky on his tower-
    ing shoulders,
Atlas whose pine-crowned head, with clouds and
    darkness encircled,
Ever is beaten by winds, is buffeted ever by
    tempests.
Snow for his shoulders has woven a mantle, and
    torrents are tumbling   250
Down from his aged chin, and his rough beard
    bristles with hoar-frost.
Here Cyllenius first down swooping on balancing
    pinions,
Rested, and bodily hence he flung himself down
    to the billows,

Like to a low-flying bird which, skimming the
        plain of the ocean,
Circles about the shores and over the fish-haunted
        ledges.   255
Thus the Cyllenean-born between earth and the
        heavens was flying,
Thus was he cleaving the air toward Libya's sand-
        covered seashore,
While he was coming from Atlas, the father of
        Maia, his mother.
Scarcely with wingéd feet hath he touched the
        skirts of the city,
When he discovers Æneas establishing castles and
        building   260
Houses anew; and there was his sword with amber-
        hued jasper
Brilliantly set; and a cloak resplendent with Ty-
        rian purple
Hung from his shoulders, the gifts which munifi-
        cent Dido had made him,
Interweaving the fabric with gold in delicate
        threadwork.
Mercury straight attacks : " Foundations of tower-
        ing Carthage,   265
Here for thy love thou art laying, and building a
        beautiful city !
Quite forgetful, alas, of thine own dominion and
        duty !
Now hath the king of the gods, who revolveth the
        sky at his pleasure,
Hastened me down unto thee from the shining
        heights of Olympus,
Sent by himself, on the wings of the wind, I am
        come with these mandates ;   270

What dost thou plan ?   With what hope dost thou
    loiter in Libya's borders ?
Yet, if no vision of glorious victory kindle thy
    spirit,
Though, for thine own renown, thou covet not labor
    and hardship,
Think on Ascanius, growing, consider the hopes of
    Iulus;
He is thine heir ; unto him falls Italy's throne as
    a birthright,   275
Aye, and the land of Rome."   Cyllenius thus hav-
    ing spoken,
Waiting for no reply, withdrew from the vision of
    mortals,
And afar off disappeared from their eyes in the
    shadowy heavens.
But, by the vision astounded, Æneas was dumb
    with amazement ;
Bristled his hair with fright, and his tongue be-
    came speechless with terror ;   280
Burning to make his escape, and the land of de-
    light to abandon,
Stunned by so great a rebuke, and Heaven's im-
    perial mandate.
But, alas ! what can he do ?   What speech can he
    risk for appeasing
Now the infuriate queen ; what words adopt for
    his prelude ?
Swiftly his wavering thoughts he despatches now
    hither, now thither,   285
Hurries them back and forth, and turns them to
    every quarter.
This, to his hesitant mind, appears the most hope-
    ful solution :

Mnestheus he calls, and Sergestus, and also in-
    trepid Serestus;
Quietly they are to order the fleet, get the men to
    the seashore,
See to the arms, and invent some excuse for their
    sudden manœuvres.   290
Meanwhile, he himself, while as yet most excellent
    Dido
Has no suspicion, nor fears that affection so strong
    can be broken,
He will discover a way, the most delicate moment
    for speaking,
And the most feasible mode of arranging the mat-
    ter.   His orders
Instantly all obey, and rejoicingly follow his
    bidding.   295
  Nevertheless the queen (who ever outwitted a
    lover?)
Fathomed their wiles, and was first to divine their
    approaching departure,
Fearful while all was safe.   To her frenzy the
    same cruel Rumor
Whispered of ships equipped, and a course already
    determined.
Breaks her distracted heart, and wandering over
    the city   300
Madly she raves like Thyas, inspired by the fran-
    tic procession,
When the triennial orgies arouse her, and Bacchus
    is calling,
When she is summoned at night by the clamorous
    voice of Cithæron.
Finally, breaking forth, she wildly reproaches
    Æneas : —

"What, perfidious man! hast thou hoped that
    a crime so atrocious   305
Thou couldst dissemble? and stealthily steal away
    from our borders?
Doth not our love constrain, nor the troth thou
    hast plighted so lately?
Nay, nor Dido doomed to a cruel death if thou
    leave her?
What! art thou building a fleet in the very heart
    of the winter?
And dost thou hasten to go on the deep while the
    north winds are raging?   310
Cruel! But what! were thy quest not an alien
    land and an unknown
Place of abode, nay, grant that thine ancient Troy
    were still standing,
Wouldst thou for Troy set sail across a tempestu-
    ous ocean?
Me dost thou flee? By these tears, by thine own
    right hand I implore thee,
(Since I myself have reserved to myself naught
    else in my sorrow,)   315
By our marriage bond, by the wedded life we have
    entered,
If I have ever well merited aught of thy love, or
    have ever
Found any grace in thy sight, oh, pity a house that
    is falling.
If there be still any place for my prayers, abandon
    thy purpose!
'T is for thy sake the Numidian kings and Libyan
    nations   320
Hate me, and Tyrians threat; for thee, and thee
    only, my honor

And the good name I bore, my only credentials to
    heaven,
These are no more! Unto whom dost thou leave
    me, while dying, my guest-friend?
Since this name alone is left to me now for my
    husband!
What shall I live for? for brother Pygmalion to
    ruin my city?   325
Or for Iarbas, the Moor, to carry me off as his
    captive?
Ah, if before thy flight, some child might have
    called me his mother,
One who should bear thy name; if I had any lit-
    tle Æneas
Playing about my hall, who might only re-image
    thy features;
I should not seem to myself so wholly deceived or
    deserted!"   330
    Thus had she spoken, but he, at the bidding of
    Jove, remained steadfast,
Eyes unmoved, and controlled the love in his heart
    with a struggle.
Few were his words at last: "O queen, that thou
    richly deservest
All and more than all thou art able to put into
    language,   334
I will never deny; I will gladly remember Elissa
While I remember myself, while my body is ruled
    by my spirit.
There is but little to say. Think not that I hoped
    to elude thee,
Fleeing by stealth; not so; nor yet have I ever
    put forward
Claim to a husband's right, or made any compact
    of marriage.

Nay, if the Fates had allowed me to order my life
    as I listed,   340
And to arrange a career in accord with mine own
    inclination,
I should have honored first the Trojan town and
    the cherished
Ashes of those I loved, and Priam's tall towers
    would be standing,
And I had raised with my hands a Troy new-built
    for the vanquished.
But, to great Italy, now, Grynæan Apollo hath
    called me ;   345
Italy is the goal ordained by the Delphic responses ;
There is my love and my home.   If the castles of
    Carthage detain thee,
Thee, a Phœnician by birth, if thou lovest thy
    Libyan city,
Prithee, if Teucrians settle Ausonian land, what
    objection
Hast thou to that ?   We, too, have a right to seek
    foreign dominions.   350
Often as Night enfolds the Earth in her dews and
    her shadows,
Oft as the glittering stars arise, my father, An-
    chises,
'Monishes me in dreams, and his troubled image
    affrights me.
Me Ascanius warns, and the wrong I am doing my
    darling,
Whom I defraud of Hesperia's throne, and his
    destined dominions.   355
Nay, 't is but now that the herald of Heaven, at
    Jupiter's bidding,
Witness ye deities twain ! — on the wings of the
    wind hath delivered

Heaven's command to me; I saw him myself in
    broad daylight

Passing within the walls; with these ears did I
    drink in his message.

Harrow no longer thy heart and mine by useless
    repining.   360

Not of my choice is Italy's quest."

    While he is speaking thus, her gaze has long
    been averted,

Wandering hither and yon; but now she looks
    him all over,

Lifting her silent eyes, and thus indignantly an-
    swers : —

" No goddess-mother was thine, nor from Darda-
    nus art thou descended,   365

Traitor ! but, bristling with crags, it was Caucasus
    gave thee thy being,

Yea, and Hyrcanian tigers encouraged thy life with
    their udders.

For, what need to dissemble ?   What worse can I
    fear in the future ?

Had he a groan for my tears ?   Did his eyes once
    soften with pity ?

Was he constrained to weep ?   Did my love arouse
    his compassion ?   370

What is there left to choose ?   Now, neither most
    powerful Juno

Nor the Saturnian Father looks on with aspect
    impartial.

Nowhere is faith secure.   I welcomed thee ship-
    wrecked and needy,

Nay, in my madness I gave thee a home and a
    share in my kingdom,

Rescued the fleet thou hadst lost, and from death I
    redeemed thy companions ;   375

Oh, I am urged by the furies of hate ! Now augur
    Apollo,
Now the Lycian omens, now even the herald of
    Heaven,   .
Sent by Jove himself, comes flying with terrible
    mandates !
This, I suppose, is the work of the gods ; this care
    is disturbing
Heaven's tranquillity ! Go ! I neither detain nor
    dispute thee !   380
Italy chase with the winds ; seek over the billows
    thy kingdom !
But, as for me, I hope, if the good gods have any
    power,
Thou mayest drink thy reward 'mid the rocks, till
    thou callest on Dido
Oft, and by name ; and, from far, with terrible
    flames I will follow ;
Ay, and when icy death shall have sundered the
    flesh from my spirit,   385
Die where thou wilt, my shade will be with thee.
    Thy crime shall be punished ;
Wretch, I shall hear, and this tidings will reach
    me in nethermost Hades."
Speaking these words, she awaited no answer, but
    rushed from the courtyard,
Fainting, avoiding his eyes, and fleeing away from
    his presence ;
Leaving him much that he feared to say, and much
    that already   390
Waited to spring from his lips. Her maidens sus-
    tained her, and bore her
Yielding form to a couch in her bridal chamber of
    marble.

Yet god-fearing Æneas, for all that he longed to
    console her,
Longed to assuage her grief, and, speaking, to
    comfort her anguish,
Groaning aloud, and shaken in mind, by the pow'r
    of his passion,   395
None the less follows the word of the god, and
    returns to his galley.
Then how the Trojans toil, and down from all
    parts of the seacoast
Drag their lofty ships, and float the oiled keels on
    the billows.
Leafy the oars they bear, and the oak rough hewn
    in the forest,
Cut in their zeal for flight.   400
See! they are hurrying forth with a rush from
    each gate of the city,
Just like an army of ants, that, prudently mindful
    of winter,
Steal a great pile of grain and lay it away in their
    garner.
Moves a black line in the field, as they carry their
    spoil through the herbage,
Over the foot-worn path; part struggling hard
    with their shoulders   405
Pushing huge kernels along; part keeping the col-
    umn in order,
Punishing all delay; the whole pathway is seeth-
    ing with labor.
What are thy feelings now, at the sight of such
    diligence, Dido!
How didst thou groan when, looking abroad from
    the top of thy castle,
Thou didst behold thy shores alive far and wide,
    and the ocean,   410

Far as thine eyes can reach, confused with so
    mighty an uproar?
Pitiless Love, unto what dost thou force not the
    spirit of mortals!
Driven again to tears, she must try him once more
    by entreaty;
And once more, as a suppliant, humble her pride
    to her passion,
Lest she should needlessly die by leaving some
    way unattempted.   415
  " Anna, thou seest them hasten all over the shore,
    as they gather
Rushing from every side, and the sails now call to
    the breezes.
See how the sailors rejoicing have covered the
    decks with their garlands!
If I have lived through the dread of this terrible
    moment of anguish,
I shall also, my sister, have strength to endure it:
    yet, Anna,   420
Grant me one boon in my grief; for only on thee
    hath this traitor
Looked with respect, and to thee hath confided his
    innermost feelings;
Thou alone knowest the time and the winning way
    to approach him.
Go, dear sister, and humbly entreat our imperious
    guest-friend.
I did not swear with the Grecians at Aulis to
    slaughter the Trojans;   425
Nor did I send out a fleet against his Pergamene
    city;
I have not troubled the ashes or shades of his
    father Anchises.

Why should his obdurate ears deny themselves to
    my pleading?
Wherefore this haste? Let him grant his poor
    queen this final concession,
Let him but wait for a prosperous flight, and for
    favoring breezes.   430
I am not asking him now to renew the old ties he
    hath broken,
Nor to abandon his beautiful Rome, and relinquish
    his kingdom;
Time, only time, do I seek, a respite and rest from
    my madness;
Time for my sorrow to teach me how they who are
    vanquished should suffer.
This do I ask as my final request: O pity thy
    sister!   435
When thou shalt grant this boon, at my death I
    will doubly repay thee."
    So she kept pleading, and such are the wailings
    her heart-broken sister
Carries and carries again; but no lamentations
    can move him;
There are no voices now to which he indulgently
    listens;
Fate stands guard, and God defends the calm ears
    of the hero.   440
And, as when Alpine winds from the north are
    struggling together,
Blowing now this way, now that, to tear from the
    earth an old oak-tree,
Strong with its centuried fibres; its foliaged
    boughs, 'mid the roaring,
Litter the earth from on high, as the trunk is
    rocked by the tempest,

Yet the tree clings to the cliff, and as high as its
    crown is uplifted   445
Into the sky, so deep are its roots toward Tarta-
    rus reaching.
So, now this way, now that way, the hero is beaten
    by ceaseless
Cries, and his mighty heart is deeply stirred with
    compassion,
Yet is his mind unmoved, and vain are the tor-
    rents of weeping.
    Verily then, dismayed by her fate, unfortunate
        Dido   450
Prays for death; she is tired of the sight of the
    arches of heaven.
Further to fix her resolve the sunlight of life to
    relinquish,
While she was laying her gifts on the altars glow-
    ing with incense,
Shocking to tell, she beheld the milk turn black
    in the chalice ;
While to polluted blood was changed the wine she
    had sprinkled.   455
This was a sight that she told to none, not even
    her sister.
Added to this, there stood in the palace a chapel
    of marble,
Raised to her husband of old, which she honored
    with wondrous devotion,
Solemnly wreathed with garlands of leaves and
    snow-white fillets.
Hence she seemed to hear the voice and the words
    of her husband   460
Calling her when dark night was enfolding the
    earth in its shadows.

Also, alone on the eaves, an owl with funereal wail-
    ing
Often complained, and prolonged her cries in long
    lamentation.
Many predictions, moreover, delivered by reverend
    augurs,
Made her afraid by their terrible warning; and
    even Æneas   465
Cruelly haunted her frenzied dreams; in her
    dream she was always
Left by herself alone, and a path she was follow-
    ing ever,
Lonely and long; for her countrymen searching
    through regions deserted,
Just as when Pentheus in frenzy beholds an army
    of Furies,
Sees two suns in the sky, and the city of Thebes
    appears double;   470
Or, as when seen in the play, Agamemnon's Ores-
    tes is haunted;
When, with torches and serpents of midnight his
    mother pursues him
While the Furies of Hell are crouching low on the
    threshold.
    Therefore, as soon as, all vanquished by grief,
    she hath welcomed the Furies,
Sentenced herself to death, and the very time and
    the manner   475
Fixed in her mind; she then, as she speaks to her
    sorrowing sister,
Hides her intent with a smile, and drives the sad
    frown from her forehead.
"Dearest, a way I have found (be glad in thy
    sister's good fortune)

Which shall restore me my own, or free me from
    love's bitter bondage.
Close to the shore of the ocean, not far from the
    region of sunset,   480
Farthest of all is the Æthiop land, where Atlas the
    mighty
Turns on his shoulder the firmament studded with
    bright constellations ;
Thence hath been brought to my knowledge a cer-
    tain Massylian priestess,
Formerly guard of the shrine of Hesperides ; she
    who provided
Food for the dragon, and watched o'er the tree
    and its consecrate branches,   485
Sprinkling the liquid honey, and drowsy juice of
    the poppy.
She professes to free any heart she may choose by
    her magic,
While she lets loose upon others anxieties many
    and grievous ;
Rivers she stops in their flow, and turns back the
    stars in their courses ;
Also she calls up the shades of the dead. You
    shall see the earth rumbling   490
Under her feet, and the ash-trees moving down
    from the mountains.
God, and thyself, dear sister, and thy dear head,
    bear me witness
Not of my own accord am I girt with the weapons
    of witchcraft.
Do thou in secret erect a pyre in the court of the
    palace,
Under the sky ; and the armor that wretch hath
    left hung in his chamber,   495

Heap thou upon it, and all of his garments, and
  also the marriage
Bed, upon which I fell, for the prophetess warns
  and commands me
Utterly to destroy all tokens of one so unfaithful.
After these words she is silent, while pallor takes
  captive her features.
Anna, however, believes not that death is disguised
  by her sister   500
Under these novel rites ; nor yet in her mind hath
  imagined
Passion so fierce, or feared aught worse than the
  death of Sychæus ;
So she obeys her commands.
    But, when a lofty pyre of timbers of oak and of
  pitch-pine
Stands in the open air in the innermost court of
  the palace,   505
Then doth the queen with bright garlands and
  boughs of funereal cypress
Wreathe it ; and lay on a couch the sword he hath
  left, and his garments,
Also Æneas in effigy ; knowing full well of the
  morrow.
Altars are standing around ; and with hair dishev-
  elled the priestess
Thunders the roll of the gods ; now Erebus call-
  ing, now Chaos,   510
Hecate, triple, and visages three of the Virgin
  Diana.
Counterfeit waters, too, of the fount of Avernus
  she sprinkles ;
Downy herbs, all cut by brazen knives in the
  moonlight,

Also are sought, whose juice is a black and viru-
    lent poison ;
Sought is the lover's charm, which away from the
    mare hath been stolen,   515
Torn from the brow of her new-foaled colt.
Dido, herself, with the meal in her purified hands
    by the altar,
One foot freed from the cords of the sandal, her
    vesture ungirdled,
Calls, at the threshold of death, on the gods and
    the prescient planets ;
Then, if there be any Power, both just and regard-
    ful, that watches   520
Lovers unequally yoked, that Power she invokes
    to avenge her.
  Now, it was night, and throughout the earth tired
    bodies were snatching
Tranquil repose, and the woods and the wild sea-
    level were quiet,
While in mid-orbit the stars roll on, and glide
    through the heavens,
While all the fields are still, the beasts, and the
    bright feathered songsters,   525
Whether they linger by limpid lakes, or whether
    they favor
Thicketed fields, in the stillness of night are cradled
    in slumber,
Soothing their cares by sleep, and their hearts for-
    getful of trouble.
Not Phœnissa, however ! Unhappy of soul, she is
    never
Lulled into sleep, nor now doth she ever, with eyes
    or with spirit   530
Welcome the night, but her cares increase, and
    her love, again rising,

Mingles its furious tide with the ebb and the flow
    of her anger.

Thus evermore she is brooding; thus ever com-
    munes with her spirit:

"What shall I do? Make trial again of my
    former admirers,

Braving their scorn? Shall I stoop to invite a
    Numidian marriage?   535

I who so often already have looked with disdain
    on my lovers?

Shall I, then, follow the Ilian fleet, and the Teu-
    crian's bidding

Unto the end? Will it help me that once they
    were saved by my favor,

And that the thought of my long ago kindness is
    gratefully cherished?

Nay, if I wished, who would suffer or take me, the
    jest of the city,   540

Into those haughty ships? Oh, lost as thou art,
    wilt thou never

Learn that the oaths of Laomedon's line are made
    to be broken?

What then? Am I to fly alone with the triumph-
    ing sailors?

Or with my Tyrians follow, surrounded by all my
    retainers?

Those, whom I scarcely was able to tear from the
    city of Sidon,   545

Back to the sea shall I drive, and bid them give
    sails to the breezes?

Nay, let me die as becomes me, and drive out my
    grief with a dagger.

Thou, overborne by my tears, thou first, my sister,
    didst burden

Me with these woes, and leave me undone at mine
 enemy's mercy.
Why had I not the right to continue my life with-
 out marriage,   550
Like the beasts of the field, and never have come
 to such trouble ?
I have not kept the faith I vowed to the shades of
 Sychæus."
Such and so great were the wailings that constantly
 burst from her bosom ;
While, in his lofty ship, Æneas, determined on
 going,
Peacefully slumbered, for all preparations were
 fully completed.   555
Him the form of the god, returning with aspect
 unaltered,
Fronted in dreams, and seemed again to utter
 these warnings.
Mercury's self he appeared in all; in his voice, in
 his color,
Even his golden hair, and the beautiful limbs of
 young manhood.
"Goddess-born ! in a crisis like this canst thou
 lengthen thy slumber ?   560
Seest thou not what perils are swiftly gathering
 round thee ?
Madman, hearest thou not the favoring breath of
 the Zephyrs ?
Dido is nursing a plot and a terrible crime in her
 bosom,
Bent upon death, and adrift on the changing tide
 of her passion.
Fleest thou not from hence with speed while speed
 may avail thee ?   565

Soon shall thine eyes behold the ocean surging with
    galleys,
Torches fiercely ablaze, and the shore one vast
    conflagration,
If, still loitering here, the light of Aurora shall
    touch thee.
Up, then, and shake off thy sloth! A creature
    inconstant and fickle,
Woman for aye!" And with this he mingled
    himself with the midnight.   570
  Then, in sooth, did Æneas, alarmed by the
    strange apparition,
Instantly start from sleep, and rally his drowsy
    companions:
" Quick! be awake, my men! together, now, quick
    to the benches!
Up with the flying sails! A god commissioned
    from Heaven
Urges to hasten our flight, and to sever the strands
    of our cables.   575
Lo! 't is the second time! Whoever thou art,
    blessed Herald,
Thee do we follow, rejoicing again to obey thy
    commandment.
Oh, be thou near us, and lead us in peace; let the
    stars in the heavens
Favor our course." He spake, and drew forth his
    sword from its scabbard.
Flashes the naked steel as he strikes the cables
    asunder.   580
Kindles each heart with fire, and together they
    tug and they struggle.
Now they have left the shore, and the sea is hid by
    their vessels.

Straining, they whirl the foam, and sweep the
    deep blue of the ocean.
  Now the new light of dawn was Aurora begin-
    ning to sprinkle
Over the earth, as she sprang from the golden
    couch of Tithonus.   585
Soon as the queen from her windows perceives
    that the morning is breaking,
Soon as she sees the fleet with sails wing and wing
    disappearing,
Sees the shore and the harbor deserted and empty
    of oarsmen,
Thrice and again she beats with her hand her
    beautiful bosom,
Tearing her golden hair, and exclaiming: "Ye
    Gods! shall this stranger   590
Thus be allowed to depart, and hold our throne in
    derision?
Will they not rush to arms and pursue from all
    parts of the city?
Are there not others to tear our boats from their
    moorings? What, ho, there!
Hither with torches! To arms! Row hard, my
    Tyrian boatmen!
What am I saying? Where am I? What mad-
    ness disorders my reason?   595
Ah, wretched Dido, at last do deeds of disloyalty
    touch thee?
Then were it meet, when thou gavest thy sceptre!
    Oh, faith and devotion!
This is the man, they say, carries with him the
    gods of his fathers!
This is the man who bore on his shoulders his age-
    stricken parent!

I could have seized him and torn him in pieces
　　　and scattered his body　　　　　　　　　600
Over the waves; or his friends, Ascanius even,
　　　have slaughtered —
Why could I not ? — and have served him up as a
　　　feast for his father !
But had the hazard of war been uncertain ? Then
　　　let it have been so.
Whom did I fear at Death's door ?　I might have
　　　set fire to his galleys,
Filling his hatches with flame ; and when with the
　　　son and the father　　　　　　　　605
I had destroyed the race, have flung myself on the
　　　embers.
O thou Sun, who searchest all deeds of the Earth
　　　with thy glory,
Also, thou Juno, who knowest and feelest these
　　　tortures of passion,
Hecate, too, who wailest by night through the
　　　streets of the city,　　　　　　　609
Yea, ye avenging fiends, ye gods of dying Elissa,
Listen to this, and vouchsafe your presence to
　　　woes that deserve it.
Listen, and hear our prayer ; and if it must cer-
　　　tainly happen
That his accursèd head reach land and float to a
　　　harbor,
If the decrees of Jove are fixed, if this goal is
　　　determined,
Yet, undone by war and the sword of a resolute
　　　people,　　　　　　　　　　　615
Banished the realm and torn from the arms of his
　　　darling Iulus,
Let him go begging for aid, and see his best and
　　　his bravest

Slain in disgrace; and when to a treacherous peace
    he hath yielded,
Let him not then enjoy a throne or the day he
    hath longed for,
But, ere it dawn, let him fall far away on the
    shore, and unburied.   620
This is my prayer; with my blood I pour this dying
    petition.
Then, O ye Tyrian men! his seed to the last gen-
    eration
Follow with hate, and send these offerings down
    to our ashes.
Neither be love nor league between these nations
    forever!
Rise from my bones in the days to come, thou
    unknown avenger!   625
Follow with fire and sword the Dardanian colo-
    nists ever!
Now, and hereafter, whenever the time and the
    power shall be granted,
Shore against opposite shore, and sea against sea,
    I invoke it, —
Sword against sword, let them fight, themselves
    and all their descendants!"
Having thus spoken, she hurried her thoughts in
    ev'ry direction   630
Seeking the speediest way to break off the life she
    detested.
Then she briefly addressed old Barce, the nurse of
    Sychæus,
For dark Death held her own in the ancient land
    of her fathers!
" Go, my dear nurse, and hither to me bring Anna,
    my sister.

Say she must hasten to sprinkle her body with
    free-flowing water,   635
Also to fetch, when she comes, the sheep and ap-
    pointed oblations;
So shall she come; and do thou bind thy temples
    with consecrate fillets.
Vows unto Stygian Jove, which I have begun in
    due order,
It is my wish to complete, and thus put an end to
    my trouble,
Also to set the torch to the pyre of Dardania's
    chieftain."   640
Quickly on this the good nurse pattered off with
    an old woman's ardor.
But, affrighted and crazed by these gruesome be-
    ginnings, poor Dido —
Eyes with a murderous gleam, under eyelids trem-
    bling and tear-stained,
Face all white at the thought of Death so swiftly
    approaching —
Burst through the doors that led to the inner
    court, and in frenzy   645
Mounted the lofty pyre and unsheathed the sword
    of Æneas,
Which, though not for this use, she had begged as
    a gift from her lover.
Here, as soon as she saw the familiar couch, and
    the garments
He had worn, she stood for a moment, weeping
    and thinking,
Then she fell on the bed, and these were the last
    words she uttered: 650
" Relics of happier days, when God and the Fates
    were indulgent,

Take this spirit of mine, and set me free from
   these troubles.

Lo, I have lived; I have finished the course that
   fate hath appointed;

Now my illustrious shade shall pass to the realms
   of the future.

I have established a glorious town; I have seen
   my own bulwarks;   655

I have avenged my husband, and punished my
   treacherous brother;

Happy, too happy, alas! if only the keel of the
   Dardan

Never had touched our shore!" Then, pressing
   her face to the pillow,

" Must we then die," she cried, " with no compen-
   sation of vengeance!

Yet, let us die! Thus! thus! we rejoice to enter
   the shadows.   660

Let him, afar on the sea, drink these flames with
   his eyes, cruel Dardan!

Yea, let him bear in his heart our death and its
   ominous tokens."

Dido hath spoken. The words are still on her lips
   when her maidens

See her sink down on the steel, see the blood foaming out round the dagger;

See her hands besprent. Then rings a loud cry
   through the lofty   665

Hall, and Rumor runs wild in the startled and
   terrified city;

Echoes the palace with groans, and the weeping
   and wailing of women;

Echoes the vaulted sky with the loud lament of
   the people,

Just as if Carthage or ancient Tyre were falling
    in ruins,
Left to the mercy of foemen, and flames were roll-
    ing in fury,   670
Leaping from home to home, and roaring from
    temple to temple.
Breathless, her sister heard, and, frantic with ter-
    ror and running,
Marring her face with her nails, and frenziedly
    beating her bosom,
Forces her way through the throng, and calls by
    name on the dying:
" Was it for this, dear heart, thou didst craftily
    beg my assistance?   675
This for me were thy pyre and thy fires and thine
    altars preparing?
What is the first complaint of my loneliness?
    didst thou despise me
For a companion in death? Hadst thou called me
    to die with thee, sister,
Lo, one anguish had ended us both, — one hour,
    and one dagger!
Have I then builded this pyre, and called on the
    gods of our fathers   680
Only that thou shouldst fall like this, — I cruelly
    absent?
Me hast thou slain, my sister; thyself, and the
    princes of Sidon;
Ended thy city, thy race! Give place, good friends,
    that with water
I may assuage her wounds, and catch the last
    breath of her spirit
Should it be flickering still!" and with this, the
    tall pyre she ascended;   -   685

Now she is folding her dying sister close to her
    bosom,
Groaning aloud, and striving to staunch the dark
    blood with her garments.
Dido endeavored to raise her heavy eyes, but, ex-
    hausted,
Fainted again, while gurgled the wound deep fixed
    in her bosom.
Thrice attempting to rise, she lifted herself to her
    elbow,   690
Thrice fell back on the couch, and sought with
    wandering glances
Light in the lofty sky, but the light only deepened
    her moaning.
    Then did omnipotent Juno, moved by her linger-
    ing anguish,
Touched by her struggle with death, send Iris down
    from Olympus,
Bidding her loose the impatient soul from the
    body that held it ;   695
For, since neither by fate, nor a death deserved,
    she was dying,
But untimely and sad, and suddenly mastered by
    passion,
Not as yet had Proserpine stolen a lock of her
    golden
Hair, or doomed her head to the gloom of Stygian
    Orcus.
Therefore on saffron wings doth Iris fly down
    through the heavens,   700
Dewy, and drawing a thousand different hues from
    the sunbeams
Crossing her pathway, and hovers right over her
    head. " Under orders

This unto Pluto I bear as a sacred gift, and re-
    lease thee
Thus, from thy body." She speaks, and severs
    the hair ; the same instant
Heat hath all vanished, and life hath passed to the
    whispering breezes.   705

BOOK V

Now in the mean time Æneas was steadfastly hold-
     ing his galleys
True to their destined course, and cleaving the
     storm-darkened billows ;
Looking back at the walls already aglare with the
     blazing
Pyre of unhappy Elissa. The cause of so great
     conflagration
None of them knew ; but the pangs of passion in-
     tense and dishonored,   5
This, and the knowledge of what may be done by
     a desperate woman,
Led the hearts of the Trojans to sad and gloomy
     foreboding.
  After their vessels had gained the deep, and land
     was no longer
Visible now, but sky all around, all round them the
     waters,
Then dark masses of cloud hung sullenly over their
     vessels,   10
Bringing night and storm, and shuddered the waves
     in the darkness.
E'en Palinurus the pilot himself called down from
     the stern-sheets :
" Ah ! why is it that clouds like these have en-
     compassed the heavens ?
Or, Father Neptune, what hast thou in store ? "
     With this he gave orders,

" Stand by the ship! To the thwarts! Give way
    with your tough oaken oar-blades ! "   15
Then, as he slanted the bellying sail to the tem-
    pest, he shouted,
" Valiant Æneas, though Jove the Creator should
    give me his promise,
I should not hope in this weather to reach one of
    Italy's harbors.
Shifted athwart our bows, the winds are rising and
    roaring
Out of the blackening west, and thickens the air
    into vapor.   20
Strength have we none to make headway against
    it, nor yet are we able
Even to hold our own ; since fate overpowers, let
    us follow,
Veering wherever she calls ; methinks, too, the
    safe and fraternal
Shores of Eryx are near, nor distant are Sicily's
    harbors,
If I remember aright in retracing the stars I have
    noted."   25
Then replied faithful Æneas : " That such is the
    will of the tempest
I have been long aware, and vain are thy strug-
    gles against it.
Change thy course with the sails ; could there be
    any haven more grateful,
Or could I choose any harbor for mooring my
    wave-wearied galleys
Rather than this which is sheltering for us our
    Dardan Acestes ;   30
Cherishing, too, in its bosom, the bones of my
    father, Anchises ? "

Having thus spoken, they make for the port, and
    favoring breezes
Fill out the sails, and the fleet is swiftly swept
    through the surges,
And to familiar shores they are brought at last
    with rejoicing.
  But from the lofty top of a far-off mountain,
    Acestes   35
Hastens with glad surprise to greet their friendly
    arrival,
Bristling about with darts, rough clad in a Libyan
    bear-skin ;
Trojan his mother; his father the god of the
    Crimisus river.
He, remembering well his ancient lineage, greets
    them ;
Gives them joy of their rescue ; receives them with
    glad rustic welcome ;   40
Ministers unto their weariness out of his friendly
    abundance.
Later, when cloudless day first scattered the stars
    at its dawning,
Then from the whole broad shore Æneas convok-
    ing his comrades
Into a listening group, with a mound for his ros-
    trum, addressed them :
" Noble Dardanidæ, sprung from the glorious
    blood of immortals,   45
Now hath an annual circle of twelve full months
    been completed,
Since we laid in the earth the ashes and bones of
    my father,
Now with the gods, and reared for his worship our
    altars of mourning.

Nay, if I err not, the day draws nigh which I shall
    forever
Reckon both sacred and sad; for such is the plea-
    sure of Heaven.   50
Were I to pass this day in Gætulian deserts, an
    exile;
Should the Argolian sea, or crowded Mycenæ de-
    tain me,
Still these yearly vows, and this solemn and orderly
    service
I should fulfil, and crown his altars with fitting
    oblations.
But, by my father's own ashes and bones to-day
    we are gathered,   55
Not, I for one believe, without divine intervention,
And, though swept from our course, we rest in a
    welcoming harbor.
Come, then, and let us together glad sacrifice do
    in his honor,
Praying for winds and permission to pay these
    annual tributes,
After our city is founded, in temples ordained for
    his worship.   60
Oxen twain unto you doth Trojan-descended
    Acestes
Offer for each of your ships; invite to the banquet
    your country's
Household gods, and the gods that our host Aces-
    tes revereth.
If the ninth morning, moreover, shall bring us a
    day of fair weather,
And if Aurora shall brighten the earth with radiant
    sunshine,   65
First I will order a race of the swift-oared Teucrian
    galleys;

Also whoever is good at a foot race, or trusts in
    his prowess
Either with dart to excel, or to win with the light
    wingéd arrow;
Whoso hath courage to enter the lists with gaunt-
    lets of rawhide;
All shall attend and expect the rewards of merited
    honor."   70
All shout aloud in applause, and bind their tem-
    ples with chaplets.
Having thus spoken, he wreathes his brow with
    his mother's own myrtle;
Elymus does the same; the same does aged
    Acestes,
Youthful Ascanius, too, and the other young men
    in due order.
Then, with a mighty host, Æneas proceeds from
    the council   75
Unto the tomb, in the midst of a thronging crowd
    of companions.
Here, duly making libation, he empties two beak-
    ers of purest
Wine, and two of new milk on the earth, and two
    that with sacred
Blood were o'erbrimming; and blossoms of purple
    he scatters, exclaiming: —
"Hail, O parent divine! Once more, all hail,
    O ye ashes   80
Vainly to me restored! Hail, spirit and soul of
    my father!
Not with thee might I search for Italy's confines
    and destined
Fields; nor, be what it may, discover Ausonian
    Tiber."

This had he said, when a huge and glittering ser-
    pent came trailing
Up from the base of the shrine seven coils and
    sevenfold spirals,   85
Gently encircling the tomb, and gliding over the
    altars.
Markings of emerald blazoned its back, and vary-
    ing tinctures
Kindled its scales with gold ; as Iris o'erarching
    the storm-cloud
Flashes back to the sun the myriad hues of the
    rainbow.
Stunned by the sight was Æneas ; yet still, in a
    lengthening column   90
Winding its sinuous way 'mid bowls and glittering
    goblets,
Lightly it lipped the feast, and harmlessly back-
    ward retreated
Under the base of the tomb, just tasting and quit-
    ting the altars.
All the more zealously now he continued the rites
    to his father,
Knowing not whether the serpent were God of the
    place, or a spirit   95
Guarding the dead.   Two lambs he offered accord-
    ing to custom,
Also a couple of swine and a pair of sable-skinned
    bullocks,
Pouring out bowls of wine, and calling aloud on
    the mighty
Soul of Anchises, whose shades were redeemed
    from Acheron's prison.
Then his companious, too, each after his means,
    with rejoicing   100

Offer their gifts, till they burden the altar ; some
  sacrifice bullocks,
Others arrange great caldrons of brass, or,
  stretched on the greensward,
Kindle a fire of coals and roast the flesh by the
  embers.
  Dawns the expected day ; already are Phaëthon's
    horses
Bearing the ninth Aurora aloft with glory un-
  unclouded.   105
Rumor, moreover, conjoined with the name of the
  famous Acestes,
Roused the neighboring people, who joyously
  crowded the seashore
Eager to gaze on the Trojans ; and some to en-
  gage in the contests.
First, in the sight of all, and ranged in the inner-
  most circle,
Prizes are shown, even tripods of sacrifice, leafy
  green chaplets,   110
Palm branches, too, for the victors, and armor, and
  garments of purple,
  Evenly dyed, and a talent of gold, and a talent of
    silver ;
While from the hilltop the trumpet announces the
  opening contest.
Chosen from all the fleet, four galleys of uniform
  oarage,
Equal also in weight, have entered the first of the
  races.   115
Mnestheus with eager crew is urging the swift-
  darting Pristis ;
" Mnestheus of Italy," soon, whence the name of
  the Memmian household ;

Gyas commands the Chimæra, which looms up
    vast as a city,
Bulky and broad and high, and Dardanian youth
    on the benches
Drive it along with oars that strike in triplicate
    measure.   120
Then Sergestus, from whom the Sergian line is
    descended,
Rides on the Centaur huge; on dark green Scylla,
    Cloanthus,
Whence thine illustrious line is traced, O Roman
    Cluentius.
    Opposite foaming shores is a rock, far away in
      the offing,
Pounded and whelmed at times by the on-rush of
    turbulent breakers,   125
When bleak northwest winds o'ercloud the stars in
    the heavens:
Silent in days of calm, it rises through slumbering
    waters
Level and smooth, a site most favored by sun-
    loving sea-gulls.
Here did father Æneas determine the goal by a
    verdant
Bough from a thick-leaved oak; that the rowers
    might know by this token   130
Whence they must make their return, and where
    their long course must be doubled.
Next they chose places by lot; and, astern on the
    decks, are the captains
Gleaming afar in gold, and the radiant beauty of
    purple,
While all the youth at the oars are crowned with
    chaplets of poplar.

Thoroughly rubbed with oil, their naked shoulders
    are gleaming.   135
Now as they sit on the thwarts, their forearms
    stretched for the oar-stroke,
Nervously waiting the signal, the quivering throb
    of their pulses
Drains their rioting hearts, and sharp is their
    hunger for glory.
Then, when the shrill-toned trumpet resounds,
    there is no hesitation ;
All shoot forth from the line ; heaven rings with
    the shouts of the oarsmen ;   140
Churned by the might of their muscular arms the
    channel is foaming ;
Parallel furrows they cut, and all the sea-level
    breaks open,
Harrowed by oars, and ploughed by the three-
    pronged beaks of the galleys.
Not with so headlong a plunge from the goal in a
    double-yoked contest
Chariots dash o'er the plain and stream out over
    the race-course ;   145
Nor over steeds so free have charioteers, leaning
    forward,
Shaken their floating reins, as they hang far over
    the whip-lash.
Then with the clapping and shouting of men, and
    cheers of well-wishers,
Ring all the groves at once ; wooded shores reëcho
    the chorus,
While the reverberant hills resound with tumultu-
    ous echoes.   150
Drawing away from the rest, in the height of the
    bustle and uproar,

Gyas darts over the waves to the front; then closely
    Cloanthus
Follows, more skilled at the oars, but the weight
    of his lumbering galley
Holding him back; in the rear, and about the same
    distance asunder,
Struggle the Centaur and Pristis to gain the bet-
    ter position.   155
Aye! and now Pristis hath won it; and now the
    huge bulk of the Centaur
Passes her vanquished, and now both vessels sweep
    onward together,
Ploughing the shallow brine in long and parallel
    furrows.
Now they were nearing the rock and making the
    turn of the goal-post,
When in the midst of the eddying waters victori-
    ous Gyas   160
Shouted aloud to Menœtes, who guided the helm
    of the vessel:
"Why art thou going so far to the right? Direct
    thy course hither;
Cuddle the shore! Let the oar-blade graze the
    ledges to larboard;
Leave the deep sea to the others!" he cries, but
    Menœtes, the helmsman,
Fearful of hidden rocks, keeps turning the prow
    to the channel.   165
"Why dost thou still go wrong? Turn back to
    the rock, O Menœtes,"
Gyas again roars out; and lo, in his wake, close
    behind him,
Sees Cloanthus dart forward, and steer in nearer
    the shore-line.

He, between Gyas's boat and the rocks that were
    sullenly roaring,
Grazing the left, wins the inside course, and sud-
    denly passing   170
Him who was first, clears the goal and glides into
    safe open waters.
Then, of a truth, great wrath blazed up in the
    young captain's marrow,
Nor were his cheeks unwet with tears, and, equally
    reckless
Both of his own good name and the safety of those
    who were with him,   174
Headlong into the sea he tumbled clumsy Menœtes.
He, then, the master himself, springs quick to the
    tiller as steersman,
While he both rallies the rowers and wrenches the
    helm to the landward.
But, as at length scarce saved from the watery
    depths, old Menœtes,
Heavy and drenched, is now clambering up the
    precipitous ledges,
Now on the sun-dried rock is seated in brine-drip-
    ping garments,   180
Him, as he fell, did the Trojans deride; they
    mocked at him swimming;
Now they are laughing again as his lungs reject
    the salt water.
Then in the two who are last, Sergestus and Mnes-
    theus, a joyous
Hope is enkindled that Gyas may now be passed as
    he lingers.
Rushes Sergestus ahead, and now to the rock is
    approaching,   185
Yet he is not in the lead by quite the length of his
    galley;

Partly ahead, part pressed by the beak of emulous
    Pristis.

But, in the midst of his boat and striding up close
    to his comrades,

Mnestheus exhorts, " Now rise ! rise, now, on your
    oars all together,

Hector's own lads, whom I chose for my friends
    when the final disaster   190

Fell on the city of Troy ; now give us a proof of
    that prowess,

Show us that spirit once more that you showed in
    Gætulia's quicksands,

Through the Ionian sea, and the hounding waves
    of Maléa !

Mnestheus covets not now to be first, nor strives
    to be victor,

Though ! — but let them succeed unto whom thou
    hast granted it, Neptune.   195

Yet it were shame to be last to return ; this dis-
    grace, O my comrades,

Vanquish, and suffer it not ! " Then they with
    their utmost endeavor

Pull till the great bronze keel is quivering under
    their oar-strokes.

Backward is driven the sea ; then hurried and
    difficult breathing

Shakes their limbs and their parching lips, and
    sweat flows in rivers.   200

Only an accident brings to the men the coveted
    honor :

For while maddened with rage Sergestus is urging
    his galley

Inwardly toward the rocks, and threading the
    treacherous channel,

On a projecting rock the luckless captain is driven.
Tremble the cliffs, and the oars on the shelving
    edge of the ledges   205
Strain and snap, and the prow hard jammed on
    the rock is suspended.
Rowers all spring to their feet; there 's delay and
    a terrible uproar;
Iron-shod poles they seize, and grasping their
    sharp-pointed boat-hooks,
Gather the splintered oars that float in the eddy-
    ing waters.
Mnestheus, however, rejoicing, and keener for very
    good fortune,   210
Under the swift-marching oars, and winds invoked
    to befriend him,
Makes for the level sea, and glides into smooth
    open water.
Yea, as a dove from a cleft in the rocks, when
    suddenly startled, —
Safe in the sheltering cliff are her home and her
    brood of sweet nestlings, —
Rises to fly to the fields, and frightened away from
    her covert,   215
Makes a great flapping of wings, then into still
    air quickly gliding,
Skims on her liquid way, nor flutters her arrowy
    pinions;
Even so Mnestheus, so Pristis herself, in her flight
    cuts the farthest
Waters, and glides along impelled by sheer force
    of momentum.   219
First he passes Sergestus, toiling hard on the lofty
Rock and the sandy shoals, and shouting in vain
    for assistance,

Learning the difficult art of rowing with oars that
    are broken.

Making for Gyas next, he challenges clumsy Chi-
    mæra;

Who, of her pilot bereft, is fain to withdraw from
    the contest.

Now at the very end, when no one is left but Clo-
    anthus,   225

Him he pursues and presses hard in a desperate
    struggle.

Then, of a truth, the din is redoubled; all shout
    to encourage

Him who pursues, and the sky reëchoes the sound
    of their cheering.

These are incensed by the thought of losing the
    fame and the glory

Already won, and are willing to barter their lives
    for their honor;   230

Those are cheered by success; they can win, for
    they seem to be winning.

Aye, and with even prows, perchance they had
    tied for the prizes,

Had not Cloanthus extended both hands to the
    ocean, outpouring

Prayers and invoking the gods with vows to grant
    his petition:

" Gods, whose realm is the sea, ye Rulers whose
    waters I traverse,   235

Joyously on this beach to your altars a glistening
    bullock

I, under bond of my vow, will pledge, and scatter
    its vitals

Over the salt sea wave, and wine will I pour in
    libation."

Heard were the words he spake by the nymphs in
    the depths of the ocean,
All the Nereid choir, the Tritons, and chaste Pan-
    opea ;   240
Nay, with his own great hand pushed Father Por-
    tunus the galley.
She than the wind more swift, more swift than the
    quick-flying arrow,
Sped away to the shore, and hid herself deep in
    the harbor.
Then did the son of Anchises, when all had been
    formally summoned,
Through the loud voice of a herald proclaim as
    the victor, Cloanthus,   245
Wreathing about his brows a crown of evergreen
    laurel ;
Also he gives to the rowers their choice of re-
    wards, whether bullocks
Three for each vessel, or wine, or a generous talent
    of silver ;
Special prizes he adds for the men who had cap-
    tained the galleys ;
Mantle of gold for the victor, surrounded by broad
    Melibœan   250
Purple in winding streams, flowing on like a double
    Mæander,
While, embroidered between, the Prince on leaf-
    hidden Ida
Wearies nimble deer with his dart and the speed
    of his running.
Life-like, as if he were breathing, Jove's eagle hath
    snatched him from Ida,
And in his crooked claws is swiftly bearing him
    upward.   255

Vainly his guardians old are spreading their palms
    to the heavens,
Vainly his furious hounds are baying the sky in
    their anger.
But unto him who has won by his valor the second
    position,
Unto this man, for his own, he gives a glittering
    corselet,
Woven with triplicate links of gold; which him-
    self as a victor   260
Stripped from Demoleus, near great Troy, where
    Simois rushes.
This he may keep as a prize and a sure protection
    in battle.
Phegeus and Sagaris, bondmen, though bracing
    their shoulders together,
Bend 'neath the weight of its manifold links, yet
    Demoleus wore it
When long since on foot he followed the scattering
    Trojans.   265
Unto the third he gives twin caldrons of brass as
    a trophy,
Skiff-patterned cups of wrought silver, moreover,
    embossed with raised figures.
Finally all had been honored, and proud of their
    gifts were departing
Having their temples adorned with fillets of Ty-
    rian purple,
When, from the merciless rock wrenched free by
    skill and hard labor,   270
Crippled by loss of oars, and bereft of one rank of
    his oarsmen,
Lo, amid jeers, without honor, Sergestus came
    driving his galley.

Just as quite often a serpent, that, caught on the
    crown of a highway,
Sidelong a brazen wheel has crossed, or a wayfarer
    fiercely
Smiting has left half killed by a stone, and man-
    gled, endeavors   275
Vainly to make its escape, describing long curves
    with its body,
Part of it angry, with eyes ablaze, and raising its
    hissing
Throat in the air, while part by its bruises disabled
    retards it,
Turning and twisting and knotting itself in its
    own convolutions ;
Rowed in a similar fashion, the lumbering boat had
    been moving ;   280
But is now spreading her sails and entering port
    with full canvas.
Glad that his vessel is saved, and rejoiced that his
    friends have been rescued,
Unto Sergestus Æneas presents the reward he has
    promised :
Pholoë, Cretan by birth, is given to him for a
    handmaid,
Skilled in the arts of Minerva, and pressing twin
    sons to her bosom.   285
   Now that this contest is closed, God-fearing
    Æneas advancing
Enters a grass-covered plain completely encircled
    by forests
Set upon curving hills ; and, cent'ring the theatre-
    valley,
There was a race-course ring, to which, with thou-
    sands around him,

Forward the hero pressed to a station commanding
    the concourse.   290
Here by prizes he fires the zeal of all who are wil-
    ling
In the swift race to contend ; and here he exhibits
    the trophies.
Trojans from every side and Sicilians come throng-
    ing together ;
Nisus the first, with Euryalus.
Noted for beauty, Euryalus, famed for his vigor-
    ous manhood ;   295
Nisus, for loyal love to the lad ; next after them
    followed
Princely Diores, descended from Priam's illustri-
    ous household.
Patron and Salius next, the one Acarnania's hero,
While the Arcadian blood of the other was traced
    from Tegæa ;
Helymus, then, a Trinacrian youth, and Panopes
    also,   300
Craftsmen in forest lore, and friends of aged
    Acestes.
Many besides there were, now lost in the gloom of
    tradition.
Stationed then in the midst, Æneas addressed them
    as follows ;
" Take these words to your hearts ; rejoice and be
    glad in this promise ;
None of this number shall go unrewarded by me
    with a guerdon ;   305
Gleaming with burnished steel, two Cretan darts
    I will give you,
Also an axe for a trophy, twin-bladed and hilted
    with silver.

This one gift is assured unto all; three prizes the
    leaders
Also shall win, and their brows shall be wreathed
    with golden-leaved laurel.
He that wins first shall receive a steed resplendent
    with trappings; 310
He that is next be graced with an Amazonian
    quiver
Filled with arrows of Thrace; a broad gold band
    runs around it,
And with a tapering jewel a buckle securely con-
    fines it;
He who is third shall depart content with this
    helmet from Argos."
Taking their place at the word, and suddenly hear-
    ing the signal, 315
Stream they forth on the track, and leaving the
    line far behind them
Sweep straight on like a storm, all eyes intent on
    the goal-post.
Nisus is first away, his body in front of all others
Flashing, more swift than the wind, yea, swifter
    than wings of the lightning.
Next unto him, but next at a well marked distance,
    there followed 320
Salius; then with a space left widely open between
    them,
Came Euryalus third.
Close is Euryalus pressed by Helymus, then right
    behind him
Flies Diores; behold! how heel with heel he is
    grazing!
Shoulder to shoulder he runs, and if only the
    course could be lengthened, 325

He would out-distance his rival, or render the vic-
tory doubtful.
Now, exhausted and near to the end of the track,
they were speeding
On to the goal itself, when Nisus, unfortunate ·
Nisus,
Slipped on some gliddery blood, which it chanced
from sacrificed bullocks
Over the ground had flowed, and thoroughly
drenched the green herbage.   330
Here, on the slippery earth, the youth already
exultant
Fails his tottering steps to hold, but plunges head-
foremost
Into the thick of the mire, and the blood of the
consecrate victims.
Yet he remembers Euryalus, nor is their friend-
ship forgotten,
For from the slime he springs against Salius heavily
striking,   335
So that he staggers and falls outstretched on the
miry arena.
Forward Euryalus flashes, and victor by favor of
friendship,
Darts to the front and flies 'mid a tumult of clap-
ping and cheering.
Helymus finishes next, and now, third victor,
Diores.
Then the whole ring of the vast amphitheatre, also
the foremost   340
Ranks of the senators, Salius fills with loud pro-
testations,
While he demands that the prize that was captured
by fraud be restored him.

Favor Euryalus saves, with the grace of his tears
    and his courage,
Worth being valued the more when it comes in a
    beautiful person.
Also Diores assists, and loudly proclaims him the
    victor;   345
For he has won the palm, and vainly attained the
    last honor,
If the return of the first unto Salius now be con-
    ceded.
Then said Father Æneas, " Young men, the deci-
    sion is final;
Safe are your prizes, and none shall disturb the
    order of merit;
Let me console the mischance of a friend un-
    touched by dishonor."   350
Speaking, he flung the skin of a huge Gætulian
    lion,
Heavy with hair and with claws of gold, around
    Salius' shoulders.
Instantly Nisus exclaimed, " If such be the meed of
    the vanquished,
If thou so pity the fallen, what fitting reward
    upon Nisus
Wilt thou bestow, who had won unchallenged the
    first of the chaplets,   355
Had not the same ill chance which Salius met
    overthrown me ? "
Then, as he spoke these words, he showed his limbs
    and his features
Stained and besprent with mire.   At his plight the
    most excellent father,
Smiling, and bidding a shield be brought, Didy-
    maon's handwork,

Taken down by the Greeks from the sacred portal
    of Neptune,   360
On the distinguished youth bestowed this illustri-
    ous trophy.
Afterward, when all races were closed and the
    prizes awarded,
" Now if any be bold, with a resolute heart in his
    bosom,
Stand and raise your hands and forearms, bound
    with the gauntlets."
Thus he exclaims, and announces a twofold reward
    for the contest ;   365
Unto the victor a bull bedecked with gold and
    with fillets ;
Also, to comfort the vanquished, a sword and a
    marvellous helmet.
Instantly, waiting for naught, gigantic and power-
    ful Dares
Lifted his head, and stood 'mid loud acclaim of the
    heroes ;
Dares, the only man who was wont to stand against
    Paris ;   370
He, too, it was by the tomb where Hector, the
    mighty, lies buried,
Smote victorious Butes, the giant, who haughtily
    boasted
Kinship with Amycus' line by descent from Bebry-
    cian princes,
Stretching him, hurt to the death, on the golden
    sand ; such is Dares
Who is now loftily lifting his head at the first note
    of battle,   375
Showing his shoulders' breadth, and his arms, one
    after the other,

Stretching haughtily forth, and beating the air in
    defiance.
Where is another to match him ?   Not one in the
    whole great assembly
Dares to confront this man, or put on the gaunt-
    lets before him.
Eagerly, therefore, and thinking that all had with-
    drawn from the contest,   ·   380
Facing Æneas he stands, and short is his limit of
    patience :
Then the left horn of the bull he seizes : " O son
    of a goddess,
Since there is none who dares to hazard his life in
    the combat,
What is the limit of waiting?   How long is it
    right to detain me ?
Bid me lead off the prize."   The Trojans, all shout-
    ing together,   385
Roar their approval, demanding the promised re-
    ward for the hero.
Then, with upbraiding, Acestes unsparingly lashes
    Entellus,
Next unto whom he reclines on the verdant couch
    of the hillside :
" O Entellus, in vain aforetime the bravest of
    heroes,
Dost thou so patiently suffer, without any contest,
    such prizes   390
Thus to be won ?   Where now is that Eryx we
    worshipped, whom vainly
Thou for thy master hast claimed ?   Where now
    is thy fame that o'ershadowed
All the Trinacrian isle, and those trophies that
    hung in thy palace ? "

Quickly he answered, " Not quenched by fear is
    my longing for glory ;

Nor my desire for praise ; but age is retarding the
    icy   395

Flow of my blood, and the sluggish currents of
    life are congealing.

Had I what once I had, and in which yon braggart
    confiding,

Vaunteth himself; were mine that youth which
    hath long since departed,

Not allured by a prize and the hope of a beauti-
    ful bullock

Would I have come ; nor now do I tarry for
    gifts ! " and thus speaking,   400

Into the midst he hurled a pair of ponderous gaunt-
    lets.

Eryx the dauntless, of yore with these had been
    wont to do battle,

Binding his hands and arms with thongs of well-
    seasoned bull's-hide.

Hearts were appalled ; seven folds of the hides of
    bulls so enormous

Stiffened in rigid coils insewn with lead and with
    iron.   405

Dares himself, above all, was confounded, and
    stoutly protested ;

E'en the brave son of Anchises eyed keenly the
    terrible weapons,

Turning over and over the ponderous coils of the
    gauntlets.

Then these words from his heart the old man flings
    in rejoinder :

" What, then, if one could have seen the arms and
    looked on the gauntlets   410

Hercules owned ; and have viewed on this very
     shore the grim battle !
Eryx once wore these arms, yes, Eryx, the son of
     thy mother ;
Still canst thou see how with blood and with brains
     they are stained and bespattered.
'Gainst the great son of Alcides with these did he
     stand ; and I used them
Long as more vigorous blood gave strength ; while
     Age, my dread rival,   415
Had not as yet grown gray, nor scattered his frost
     on my temples.
But, if your Dares of Troy object to these arms of
     our choosing,
If good Æneas approve, and Acestes, my sponsor,
     be willing,
Make we the fight more fair ; I spare you the
     bull's hide of Eryx ;
Banish thy fears ; and thou must relinquish those
     Ilian gauntlets."   420
Having thus spoken, he flung from his shoulders
     the folds of his mantle ;
Then, the huge joints of his limbs, his mighty
     frame and great muscles
Baring, gigantic he stood in the midst of the sandy
     arena.
Then did Father Æneas bring gauntlets that
     matched one another,
Binding with equal arms the hands of both the
     contestants.   425
Instantly each stood forth, with body erect, and on
     tiptoe ;
High aloft in the air his arms each dauntlessly
     lifted ;

Back, far away from the stroke, their towering
    heads they are tossing;
Hands intermingle with hands; they are daring
    each other to combat;
That one, the better of foot, on the quickness of
    youth is relying;   430
This one excels in the bulk of his limbs, but his
    knees' tardy hinges
Fail, and laboring breath his giant body con-
    vulses.
Many blows in vain do the champions thrust at
    each other;
Many on echoing ribs they rain; and loudly they
    thunder
Full on the chest, while hands about ears and
    temples are playing   435
Heavy and fast, and jaws 'neath terrible buffets
    are cracking.
Ponderous stands Entellus, and, fixed in the same
    alert posture,
Only with body and vigilant eye is avoiding the
    lunges;
Dares, like one who beleaguers a towering city
    with engines,
Or with tented array besieges a hill-crowning for-
    tress,   440
Skilfully tries now these and now the other ap-
    proaches,
Circling the ring, and attacking in vain with va-
    ried manœuvres.
Rising against him, Entellus outstretched his right
    hand and upraised it
High overhead; but his foe, as the stroke came
    down from above him,

Quickly foresaw, and escaped by a sudden swerve
    of his body. 445

Wasting his strength on the air, Entellus, un-
    touched by his rival,

By his own ponderous bulk overweighted, pitched
    heavily forward,

Falling to earth, as oft upon Mount Erymanthus
    or Ida,

Pine-trees, hollow and huge, have suddenly fallen
    uprooted.

Teucrian men and Trinacrian youth spring up in
    confusion; 450

Rises a shout to the sky, and Acestes is first to
    run forward,

And in compassion lift up from the earth the
    old friend of his boyhood.

But, unhurt by his fall, and nothing daunted, the
    hero

Keener returns to the fight, and arouses his
    strength by his fury;

Shame and conscious worth are also enkindling
    his spirit; 455

Fiercely o'er all the plain he drives the fugitive
    Dares;

Now and again his blows with right hand and left
    are redoubled.

Neither delay nor rest; with strokes as incessant
    as hailstones

Rattling from cloud to roof, with either hand is
    the hero

Ceaselessly buffeting Dares and driving him o'er
    the arena. 460

Father Æneas, however, imposing a limit to an-
    ger,

Also restraining Entellus from venting his violent
    temper,
Instantly ended the fight, and rescued discomfited
    Dares,
Comforting him with words, and thus he kindly
    addressed him :
" Ill-fated man ! What madness so great hath
    o'ermastered thy spirit !   465
Recognizest thou not the might and displeasure of
    Heaven ?
Yield to the god." He spake, and speaking ended
    the contest.
Faithful young comrades, however, lead Dares
    away to the galleys,
Dragging his faltering knees, his head all listlessly
    swaying,
Spitting thick gore from his mouth, and teeth with
    blood intermingled.   470
Then they are summoned back to receive the sword
    and the helmet,
While they resign to Entellus the bull and the
    glory of conquest.
Then cried the victor, elated in mind, and proud
    of his bullock,
" Child of a Goddess, and Teucrians all, be ad-
    vised by this token
Both what strength was mine ere age had enfee-
    bled my body,   475
And from what death redeemed ye have rescued
    the life of this Dares."
Thus having spoken, he stood directly confronting
    the bullock,
Which, as the gift of the fight, was standing be-
    side him ; then backward

Raising his hand on high, he dashed the terrible
    gauntlet
Midway the horns, through the skull, and crushed
    was the brain underneath it.   480
Staggered the bull, and fell, head foremost, trem-
    bling and lifeless.
Standing above it, such words as these he poured
    from his bosom,
" Better than Dares' death, this life do I pay thee,
    O Eryx!
Here, as a victor, henceforth resigning my art and
    my gauntlets."
    Straightway Æneas invites to contend with the
    swift-flying arrow   485
Those who may chance to be willing, and fixes the
    order of prizes.
Also with powerful hand, a mast from the ship of
    Serestes
Raises, and down from its top suspends a flutter-
    ing pigeon,
Held by a floating cord; at this they may level
    their arrows.
Gather the men; and the lots in a brazen helmet
    are mingled.   490
Then doth Hippocoön, Hyrtacus' son, amid shouts
    of approval,
Draw the first lot for himself, and win the first
    place in the contest.
Next him Mnestheus comes, the winner just now
    of the boat-race,
Mnestheus, around whose brow still circles the
    green of the olive;
Third is Eurytion, brother to thee, O Pandarus
    mighty;   495

Thou who in days of old, when bidden to break
    off the treaty,
Into the midst of the Greeks wert first to deliver
    thy weapon ;
Last, in the depths of the helmet, Acestes alone is
    remaining,
Daring to try with his own right hand the feats of
    young manhood.
Now their curving bows they are bending with
    powerful muscles,   500
Each for himself, aud each draws forth a shaft
    from his quiver.
First flew the arrow of Hyrtacus' son from the
    whistling bow-string
Far through the sky, and cleft the fleeting breezes
    asunder ;
Straight to the mast it flew, and deep in the wood
    was embedded.
Trembled the mast, and the bird was frightened
    and fluttered her pinions ;   505
Echoed the hills and shore with the sound of up-
    roarious cheering.
Mnestheus next, with bended bow stepped eagerly
    forward,
Aiming aloft with eyes as tensely strained as his
    bowstring ;
Yet the unfortunate man hath failed of sending
    his arrow
Into the bird ; but the knot and the hempen cord
    he hath broken,   510
Fastened by which she hung by her foot from the
    towering masthead.
Forth on the wind she fled, to the shelter of clouds
    and of darkness ;

Straightway then, as an arrow already he held on
 his bow-string,
Strained for the shot, did Eurytion pray to his
 brother to help him,
Watching the dove as she flew through the open
 sky with a joyous   515
Beating of wings; then pierced her under the
 darkening storm-cloud.
Dying she fell, and left her life in the spaces of
 heaven,
While in her breast, as she dropped, she brought
 down the death-dealing arrow.
Only Acestes remained, but the prize was already
 another's;
Yet high into the air the old man launches an arrow,   520
Proud to exhibit his skill, and the sounding twang
 of his bowstring.
Suddenly then do our eyes behold a marvellous
 portent,
Pregnant with fate: the event soon afterward
 taught us its meaning;
All too late did the pitiless augurs interpret the
 omen;
For, as through cloud and rain the arrow was flying, it kindled,   525
Marking its track with fire; then vanished from
 sight in the heavens,
Wholly consumed; as stars, at times, when loosed
 from their stations,
Gliding across the sky, leave fiery furrows behind
 them.
Heroes of Troy and Trinacria stand bewildered
 and awe-struck,

Supplicating the gods; and even most noble
    Æneas,   530
Recognizing the sign, embraces exultant Acestes,
Loads him with generous gifts, and utters these
    words for his comfort:
"Take them, O father; for thee the great king of
    Olympus hath destined
No chance honor to gain from an omen so signal
    and joyous.
Thou shalt receive this gift, once owned by aged
    Anchises,   535
Even this cup, wrought in sculptured relief, which
    Cysseus, the Thracian,
Long ago gave to Anchises, my father, a gift of
    rare value,
Ever to keep as his own as a token and pledge of
    affection."
Having thus spoken, he wreathed his brows with
    evergreen laurel,
And, before all the rest, proclaimed as first victor
    Acestes.   540
Nor did noble Eurytion envy his honor and glory,
Though he alone had brought the dove from the
    depths of the heavens.
Next to share the awards was he who had severed
    the fast'nings;
Last was he who had pierced the mast with his
    swift flying arrow.
Father Æneas, however, the games not yet being
    ended,   545
Summoning Epytus' son, the tutor of beardless
    Iulus,
Also his friend, confides to his faithful ear these
    directions:

"Hasten," he whispers, " and tell Ascanius, if he
    be ready,

Having his line of boys prepared, and the drill of
    his horsemen

Planned, to deploy his troop, and exhibit himself
    in his armor,   550

Here by his grandsire's tomb." Then he orders
    the throng of spectators

All to retire from the length of the course, that
    the plain may be vacant.

Forward the boys march out, and, under the eyes
    of their parents,

Gleam in an even line on their bridled steeds ; and
    advancing,

All the Trinacrian youth and the Trojans admire
    and applaud them.   555

Each has his forehead enwreathed by a chaplet
    according to custom ;

Each is bearing two spears of cornel-wood headed
    with iron ;

Polished quivers by part are borne on their shoul-
    ders, and pliant

Links of twisted gold fall over their necks and
    their corselets.

Three are the troops of horse, and three their
    curvetting leaders ;   560

Then there are twice six boys, who, following after
    each captain,

Gleam in divided bands with the glory of uni-
    formed marshals.

One of the joyous divisions of youth young Priam
    is leading ;

Bearing his grandsire's name ; thy glorious son, O
    Polites ;

Destined to found an Italian line; his mount is a
    Thracian   565
Steed, all dappled with white; there are glimpses
    of white on his forefeet;
And, as he tosses his head, there's a gleam of white
    on his forehead.
Atys is next, whence Rome derives the Attian
    household:
Little was Atys, and dearly beloved by little Iulus.
Last, but surpassing them all in beauty of form,
    comes Iulus,   570
Riding a Tyrian horse which beautiful Dido had
    sent him,
Ever to keep as a proof and pledge of her loving
    affection.
By the Trinacrian steeds of aged Acestes the other
Youths are borne.
Tremble the anxious boys, and the Trojans receive .
    them with plaudits,   575
Glad to behold in their faces the looks of their gray-
    headed fathers.
After they joyously wheel on their horses around
    the arena
Under the eyes of their friends, Epytides then
    from a distance
Utters the signal — " Attention! " and gives a
    sharp crack with his whip-lash.
Then, into equal bands by threes the troopers di-
    viding,   580
March in diverging lines; and these, when the
    order is given,
Wheel their courses again, and charge with threat-
    ening lances;
Then fresh sallies they make, again to new onsets
    returning,

Rushing together from far, and wheeling in intri-
  cate circles,
Forming a picture of war, a portrayal of actual
  battle.   585
Now they expose their backs in flight, then, turning their weapons,
Take the attack, and now sweep onward in peaceful procession.
Just as in lofty Crete the Labyrinth once had an
  entrance
Fashioned with windowless walls, and a blind and
  treacherous pathway
Branching a thousand ways, where a slight and
  unmarked deviation   590
Baffled return, and confused all signs that were
  trusted for guidance;
So, interweaving the lines of their marching, the
  sons of the Trojans
Circled in mazes of flight, intermingled with mimic
  encounters;
Not unlike dolphins that cleaving the liquid Car-
  pathian waters,
Swim through the Libyan sea, disporting themselves in the billows.   595
These evolutions and games Ascanius first reëstab-
  lished
After he girded the town of Alba Longa with
  ramparts,
Teaching the primitive Latins to keep them alive
  in the fashion
He himself knew as a boy, with Troy's young
  chivalry round him:
Alba then taught the same sport to her children,
  and, centuries later,   600

Rome in her glory revived it to honor the fame of
    the fathers.

Still is the game called " Troy ; " still " Trojan "
    the band of young troopers.

Thus far were carried the games in the name of
    his deified father.

    Treacherous Fortune then first broke her faith
    with the Trojans.

While at the tomb they are paying their homage
    with varying contests,   605

Down to the Ilian fleet, from heaven, Saturnian
    Juno,

Full of her wiles (for insatiate still was her an-
    cient resentment),

Iris despatches, and breathes forth breezes to has-
    ten her going.

She o'er the radiant arch of her thousand-hued
    rainbow is speeding,

Coursing the dazzling track, a swift but invisible
    maiden.   610

Now the vast throng she views ; now, sweeping the
    shore with her vision,

Sees that the port is deserted ; and notes that the
    fleet is unguarded,

While, far away on the lonely beach, the Ilian
    matrons,

Mourning apart for Anchises lost and weeping
    together,

All gaze forth on the deep. " Alas ! what wastes
    for the weary ! "   615

" So much sea yet left ! " is the cry of each wo-
    man among them.

Home is their prayer ; they are tired of endur-
    ing the toil of the ocean.

Therefore into their midst, and not without inkling
    of evil,

Iris, doffing the face and the garb of a goddess,
    is hasting.

Beroë aged, she seems, Ismarian Doryclus' good-
    wife ;   620

For he could formerly boast of nobility, honor, and
    children.

Thus then, bearing herself 'mid the throng of Dar-
    danian matrons,

" Wretched women," she cries, " whom no Greek
    hand in the battle

Dragged unto death in sight of the walls of our
    country !   O Nation,

Destined to sorrow, to what sad end hath Fortune
    reserved thee !   625

Now, since the sacking of Troy, the seventh sum-
    mer is speeding,

While, after traversing seas and lands, and so
    many cruel

Rocks, and changing skies, we are fated to chase
    o'er the boundless

Waters our fugitive Italy, fated to toss on the
    billows.

Here is the country of Eryx our kinsman ; here
    friendly Acestes ;   630

Who, then, forbids us to build and give to our
    people a city ?

O my country — my gods, in vain from the en-
    emy rescued,

Shall not a town, after all, be named for our Troy ?
    Shall we never

Look upon Simois more, or Xanthus, the rivers of
    Hector ?

Nay! but follow with me ; let us burn these ships
    of disaster !   635
For unto me in a dream the shade of Cassandra
    the prophet
Seemed to give flaming brands; ' It is here your
    Troy must be sought for ;
Here is your home ! ' she cried, and now doth the
    time require action ;
Falter not thus forewarned. Behold four altars
    of Neptune !
Here doth the god himself provide both torches
    and spirit."   640
Speaking these words, she first caught up a threat-
    ening firebrand,
And, with uplifted arm, high whirling the glitter-
    ing fagot,
Hurled it with all her force. Aroused were the
    souls of the matrons ;
Hearts all astounded, till one, the eldest of all the
    assembly,
Pyrgo, the royal nurse of so many children of
    Priam,   645
Shouted, " Not Beroë this ; not this, O matrons,
    the Rhœtian
Consort of Doryclus ; mark these tokens of beauty
    celestial !
Look at those radiant eyes where flashes the soul
    of a goddess !
Mark ye her face, and the sound of her voice, and
    her manner of walking !
It is but now that I myself left Beroë grieving 650
That she alone is, by illness, debarred from the
    joy of this service,
Nor is permitted to render Anchises his merited
    honors."

These were her words.

Yet, for a time undecided, the matrons with eyes
    of abhorrence

Gazed on the ships, and were torn 'twixt a pitiful
    love for their present   655

Haven of rest, and desire for the realms to which
    destiny called them;

But, as on balancing wings the goddess arose
    through the heavens,

Sweeping under the clouds on the mighty arch of
    the rainbow,

Then indeed, by the omen astounded, and goaded
    by madness,

All, with loud cries, begin snatching the fire from
    the holiest altars;   660

Others the shrines despoil, and garlands, and fil-
    lets, and firebrands

Hurl in a shower; and the Demon of Fire, un-
    checked in his fury,

Sweeps over benches and oars, and the painted fir
    of the galleys.

Swift to Anchises' tomb, and through the wedged
    rows of spectators,

Eumelus carries the news that the ships are on
    fire; and the Trojans   665

See for themselves black clouds of smoke uproll-
    ing behind them.

Then, as Ascanius joyed to lead his manœuvering
    troopers,

So was he first to dash on horseback swift to the
    troubled

Camp; nor, stricken with fear, are his guardians
    able to check him.

"What new madness is this? Whither now,
    whither now are ye tending?   670

Ah, wretched women, not foes nor a hostile en-
    campment of Argives,
But your own hopes ye burn.   Behold it is I, your
    Iulus ! ''
Then he tears from his head and flings at their
    feet the light helmet,
Covered by which he was urging in sport the
    counterfeit battle.
Hastens Æneas now, now hasten the bands of the
    Trojans.   675
But in their terror the women are scattering over
    the seashore
Hither and yon, and away into caverns and forests
    are stealing
Whithersoever they may; they shrink from the
    deed and the daylight;
Contrite, they welcome their friends, and Juno is
    cast from their bosoms.
But not for that do the flames lay aside their in-
    tractable fury ;   680
Still, far under the water-logged timbers the
    smouldering oakum
Lives, and lazy smoke pours forth, and the fire,
    crawling onward,
Gnaws at the hull, and death eats into the heart
    of the vessel ;
Nor is heroic toil and the pouring of water availing.
Rending his vesture then from his shoulders, god-
    fearing Æneas   685
Stretched forth his hands in prayer, and called on
    the gods for assistance.
" Jove, thou omnipotent ! liveth there yet even one
    of the Trojans
Not in thy sight abhorred, if thine ancient com-
    passion regardeth

Human distress at all, O father, vouchsafe that
 our vessels
'Scape from the flames ; and from ruin redeem the
 frail cause of the Trojans ; 690
Or, as naught else is left, by a bolt of thy merciless thunder
Grant the release of death, and here by thy hand
 let me perish."
Scarce had he uttered these words, when a storm
 in strange fury descended,
Black with torrents of rain ; and the lofty hills
 and the lowlands
Tremble with thunder; and clouds come rushing
 over the heavens 695
Swollen with rain, and exceedingly black with
 southerly tempests.
Filled from above are the ships, and drenched are
 the half-consumed timbers,
Till the last smouldering flame is extinguished,
 and all of the galleys,
All with the loss of four, are rescued from cruel
 destruction.
 Father Æneas, however, o'ercome by the bitter
 misfortune, 700
Shifted his burden of care now this way now that
 in his bosom,
Pondering whether, unheeding the fates, it were
 better to settle
Here in Sicilian fields, or struggle for Italy's har-
 bors.
Then did old Nautes, to whom alone Tritonian
 Pallas
Destiny had revealed, and had rendered him fa-
 mous for wisdom, 705

Teach by these oracles either what Heaven's great
    anger portended,
Or the appointed course which the order of fate
    was demanding,
And with words like these began to encourage
    Æneas:
" Goddess-born, whithersoever our destiny leads,
    let us follow;
Happen what may, we must conquer each trial by
    patient endurance.   710
Here thou hast Dardan Acestes whose lineage links
    him with Heaven;
Take him to share in thy counsels; enlist him in
    cordial alliance;
Leave to his care all those who survive the lost
    ships, and surrender
All who are faint in thy cause, and weaned from
    thy great undertaking;
Also the aged men, and the matrons outworn by
    the voyage;   715
Pick out moreover all those that are feeble, and
    fearful of danger,
And in these lands let all the disheartened estab-
    lish a city,
Which they shall call, if the name be allowed
    them, the city Acesta."
    Then, of a truth, aroused by these words of his
    aged companion,
Swiftly wandered his mind through all his haras-
    sing problems.   720
Meanwhile, chariot-borne, dark Night was enfold-
    ing the heavens;
Gliding then from the sky, the form of his father
    Anchises

Seemed of a sudden to breathe on the air these
    voicings of counsel :

"O my son, ever dearer than life, while life was
    remaining,

O my son, sore tried by Ilium's fatal disasters, 725

Herald am I from Jove, who hath warded the
    flames from thy galleys,

And from the heavenly heights hath looked at last
    in compassion ;

Heed the most wise advice which reverend Nautes
    hath given ;

Chosen youth and the bravest of hearts into Italy
    carry.

Desperate peoples of barbarous breeding, in La-
    tium's borders 730

Thou must subdue ; and yet the mansions infernal
    of Pluto

First thou must visit, my son, and through the
    dark depths of Avernus

Seek for a meeting with me ; for me neither Tar-
    tarus curséd

Holds, nor its mournful shades ; but the blessed
    abodes of the righteous,

These are my home, and Elysium ; hither the pure-
    hearted Sibyl, 735

Freely shedding the blood of her dusky herd, shall
    conduct thee ;

Here all thy progeny thou shalt behold, and the
    city vouchsafed them.

Meanwhile, fare thee well ; damp Night from the
    sky is receding,

Pitiless Day with his panting steeds is breathing
    upon me."

Speaking, he vanished like smoke in the shadowy
    mist of the morning. 740

"Whither?" Æneas exclaims, "ah, whither so
    soon dost thou hasten?
Whom dost thou fear? or who forbids thee to wait
    my embraces?"
Having thus spoken, he·fans to a flame the slum-
    bering embers,
Honoring on his knees both Pergamene Lar and
    gray Vesta's
Chapel with sacred meal, and a casket o'erbrim-
    ming with incense.   745
   Straightway he summons his comrades, Acestes
    first, and discloses
Both the commandment of Jove and the words of
    his well-beloved father,
Also the purpose on which his mind was now fully
    determined.
Nothing delayed his plans, and Acestes refused
    not his bidding.   ·
Then they enroll for the town the matrons, and set
    off the people   750
Willing to stay, even all who were fired by no
    lofty ambition.
Then they replace the thwarts, and renew in the
    vessels the timbers
Charred by the fire; and refurnish the galleys
    with oars and with cordage.
Scant is their number, but brave are their hearts
    and ardent for warfare.
Meanwhile Æneas defines the bounds of a town
    with a furrow;   755
Homes he allots, and the town calls Ilium; while
    the surrounding
District is Troy; and Acestes, the Trojan, rejoices
    to rule it,

Founding a forum, and publishing laws to the
    council of fathers.

Then, near the stars, on the summit of Eryx, a
    temple is builded

Unto Idalian Venus ; and over the tomb of An-
    chises   760

There is a priest installed, and a grove, far hon-
    ored, is planted.

  Now for nine days all the people have feasted,
    and knelt at the altars

Paying their vows ; light winds have smoothed the
    face of the waters,

And once more the freshening breeze is calling
    them seaward.

Over the winding shore arises a loud lamenta-
    tion.   765

They are delayed for a night and a day in parting
    embraces ;

Even the matrons, now, and they to whom lately
    the ocean

Seemed so fearful a sight, and its name too fright-
    ful to utter,

Wish to go on, and are ready to bear all the bur-
    dens of exile.

Kindly Æneas with comforting words consoles
    them, and, weeping,   770

Unto the care of Acestes, their common kinsman,
    commends them.

Then he commands them to sacrifice three young
    bullocks to Eryx ;

Unto the Weather a lamb ; and, at last, to unfas-
    ten the cables.

He himself, crowning his head with leaves fresh
    plucked from the olive,

Standing aloft on the prow, upraises a goblet, and
    sprinkles   775
Over the salt waves wine, and the inward parts of
    the victims.
Springing astern, a breeze arises to prosper their
    voyage.
Striking with emulous oars, his comrades are sweep-
    ing the billows.
  Meanwhile doth Venus, tormented by cares, take
    counsel with Neptune ;
Pouring forth from her breast this torrent of bitter
    complaining :   780
" Juno's pitiless wrath, and her ne'er-to-be-sated
    resentment,
Force me, O Neptune, to sink to the lowest depths
    of entreaty ;
Her, neither lapse of time, nor any devotion ap-
    peases ;
Nor is she stilled by fate, nor humbled by Jupi-
    ter's mandate.
'T is not enough with unspeakable hate to have
    ravished their city   785
Out of the heart of the Phrygian race ; to have
    dragged through all tortures
All that is left ; she pursues e'en the ashes and
    bones of the nation
After its death. Ask her for the cause of so
    merciless anger.
Thou wast thyself a late witness for me in the
    Libyan waters
What a commotion she raised ; on a sudden com-
    mingling with heaven   790
All the wide seas and straits in vain with her blus-
    tering tempests.

This she hath dared in realms of thine own.

Lo, she hath even destroyed their ships by her
    wicked devices,

Foully seducing the matrons of Troy, and, through
    loss of their vessels,

Forced them on unknown shores to abandon their
    friends and companions.   795

Still there is this to ask, that over thy billows in
    safety

They may be suffered to sail, and reach the Lau-
    rentian Tiber,

If I seek only our own; if fate still concedes us
    that city."

Then the Saturnian lord of the deep made answer
    as follows:

"Every right hast thou to have faith in the sea,
    Cytherea,   800

Whence thou derivest thy line. I, too, have de-
    served it, for often

I have rebuked the wrath and the fury of sky and
    of ocean,

While upon land, no less, let Xanthus and Simois
    witness,

I have protected Æneas, thy son; when Achilles,
    pursuing,

Forced to the wall of the city the terrified bands
    of the Trojans,   805

Gave many thousands to death, and the surfeited
    rivers were groaning,

Nor could the Xanthus discover its way, or roll
    itself onward

Into the sea; then I, as he struggled with mighty
    Achilles,

Rescued Æneas, o'ermatched in strength and less
    favored by Heaven,

Hiding him in a cloud; although I had rather
    have levelled   810
All the defences of perjured Troy that my hands
    had erected.
Still do I cherish the same good will; no longer be
    troubled;
He shall in safety attain the Avernian port thou
    desirest;
Only one man shall he lose, drawn down in the swirl
    of the waters;
One for many shall die."   815
When by these words he hath soothed the gladden-
    ing heart of the goddess,
Yokes the father his steeds with gold, and fits to
    his coursers
Foaming bridles, and then, with the reins all
    streaming before him,
Light in his azure car he flies o'er the crests of
    the billows.
Sink the waves to rest, and, under his thundering
    axle,   820
Calm grows the face of the deep; clouds fly from
    the spaces of heaven;
Lo, then a changeful train of huge cetacean mon-
    sters,
Glaucus's ancient choir; Palæmon, the offspring
    of Ino;
Also the Tritons swift, and all the retainers of
    Phorcus;
Thetis and Melite marshal the left, and fair Pan-
    opea,   825
Spio and Thalia next, Cymodoce, too, and Nesæa.
    Now, in its turn, sweet joy steals into the heart
    of Æneas

Harassed so long by care ; all masts he bids to be
    quickly
Raised, and sails unfurled and hoisted home to the
    cross-trees.
All together tack ship, and veering the billowy
    mainsail   830
Starboard and port by turns, they shift the taper-
    ing yardarms
Over and back ; and the fleet is borne by favoring
    breezes.
Foremost of all, Palinurus was leading the closely
    ranked column,
Signals set for the others to follow the course of
    his galley.
Now, moreover, had mist-laden night to the zenith
    of heaven   835
Nearly attained, and the crews, outstretched on the
    hard rowing-benches
Under their oars, were sunk in the peaceful aban-
    don of slumber,
When, from the star-studded heavens the shadowy
    Dream-god descending,
Parted the yielding air, and scattered the fugitive
    shadows,
Seeking for thee, Palinurus, and bringing thee,
    guiltless of evil,   840
Evil suggestions in dreams ; and aloft on the
    stern of thy galley,
Perched in the semblance of Phorbus, he opened
    his lips and addressed thee :
" Iasides Palinurus, the sea of itself bears thy
    vessels,
Steadily breathes the wind ; an hour of repose is
    vouchsafed thee ;

Lay down thy head, and steal thy wearied eyes from
    their labor.   845
I myself, in thy stead, will relieve thee awhile
    from thy duties."
Scarcely raising his eyes, Palinurus returns him
    this answer :
"Biddest thou me not heed the face of the sea
    when it slumbers ?
Watch not the sleeping waves ?   Wouldst have
    me rely on these tokens ?
Shall I, indeed, entrust Æneas to treacherous
    breezes ?   850
I, so often deceived by the snare of a cloudless
    horizon ? "
Such was the answer he gave, and clinging fast to
    the tiller,
Nowise released his hold, and kept his eyes fixed
    on the planets.
Lo, then, over his brows a branch with the waters
    of Lethe
Dripping, and drugged with death, the god is
    drowsily waving,   855
Setting the tired eyes free in despite of the pilot's
    resistance.
Scarcely had slumber surprised and relaxed the
    limbs of the helmsman,
When the incumbent god overpowered him, and
    hurled him down headlong
Into the limpid waves, with part of the stern and
    the tiller
Torn from the ship, and often in vain calling out
    to his comrades.   860
He himself swiftly arose through the yielding air
    on his pinions.

None the less safely the fleet runs its course o'er
    the face of the waters,
Fearlessly forward borne, as father Neptune had
    promised.
Now, as still adrift, it was nearing the rocks of the
    Sirens,
Direful of old, and white with the bones of num-
    berless victims,   865
Hoarsely and far the rocks incessant re-echo the
    surges.
Soon as the father perceives that the pilotless ves-
    sel is drifting,
He himself guides her course through the midst
    of the night-darkened waters,
Frequently sighing, and grieved at heart by the
    fate of his comrade.
"Ah! too sure of a sky serene and an ocean un-
    troubled,   870
Stark on an unknown shore, Palinurus, thou liest
    unburied."

BOOK VI

SPEAKING these words with tears, and giving free
    rein to his vessels,
Safely he glides at last to the shore of Chalcidian
    Cumæ.
Seaward they turn their prows; the stubborn
    tooth of the anchor
Firmly secures the ships; curved sterns are fring-
    ing the shore-line.
Then the young men in troops leap eagerly down
    from the galleys   5
On the Hesperian strand. Some search out the
    sparks that lie hidden
Deeply in veins of flint; some plunge into forest
    and jungle
Haunted by beasts of prey, and bring tidings of
    rivers discovered.
Faithful Æneas, however, ascends to the heights
    where Apollo
Dwells, and adventures the gloom of the dread
    unapproachable Sibyl,   10
Even the awful abode of her whom the Delian
    prophet
Fills with his own great soul, and the gift of in-
    spired divination.
Now they draw nigh to the groves and golden halls
    of Diana.
    Dædalus, fleeing the kingdom of Minos, — so
      runs the tradition, —

Trusting himself on swift and adventurous wings
    to the heavens,   15
Flew through the trackless sky toward the glim-
    mer of frosty Arcturus,
Never arresting his flight till he gained the Chal-
    cidian mountain.
Here, first restored to the earth, his feathery oar-
    age, O Phœbus,
Unto thyself he vowed, and built thee a marvel-
    lous temple ;
Carved on its gate is the death of Androgeos;
    then, with what pathos,   20
Stand the Athenians, doomed to surrender in
    yearly atonement
Maidens and youths, twice seven; behold the
    dread urn standing empty !
Darkly companioning this, looms the island of
    Crete from the ocean.
Here is the mad and incestuous passion of Pasi-
    phæ pictured,
Here its unnatural fruit, that monster half brute
    and half human;   25
Darkly the Minotaur stands monumental of name-
    less dishonor.
Here, too, that marvellous maze with its hopelessly
    intricate windings ;
Hopelessly ? Nay, for the king hath pitied his
    love-stricken daughter,
And hath himself resolved the bewildering plan
    of the palace,
Guiding her lover's return by a thread; thou,
    Icarus, also,   30
Largely hadst shared in a work so grand, had
    sorrow permitted.

Twice he essayed in gold to picture thy cruel mis-
     fortune ;
Twice fell the father's hand. And thus they
     might long have continued
Scanning each scene in turn; but, lo ! their her-
     ald, Acestes,
Timely appeared, with Deiphobe, daughter of
     Glaucus, and priestess   35
Both of Diana and Phœbus, who spake these
     words to Æneas :
"Not such sights as these the present hour is
     demanding !
Now from the virgin herd to slaughter seven bul-
     locks were better,
Also as many lambs, selected according to cus-
     tom."
Thus she addressed the king, — nor delayed was
     the sacrifice ordered.   40
Then to her lofty abode the prophetess summons
     the Trojans.
   Vast is the cavern hewn in the side of the moun-
     tain of Cumæ.
Pathways an hundred are there, wide arching, and
     portals an hundred,
Whence, through an hundred mouths, the Sibyl's
     responses are uttered.
Them, at the threshold, the virgin arrests: "To
     question the future,   45
Now is the time. The god! behold the god!"
     and, thus crying,
Suddenly faces the gate, herself nor in feature nor
  ·   color ;
Kempt are her tresses no more; she is gasping,
     her bosom is heaving ;

Swells with a frenzy her passionate soul, and tow-
    'ring above them,
And with no mortal voice, for the god is now
    breathing upon her   50
Nearer and still more near; "Dost halt in thy
    vows and petitions,
Trojan Æneas," she cries; "Art silent? Then
    never the mighty
Mouths of this awful shrine shall open;" and,
    thus having spoken,
Ceased, and an icy chill unnerved the strong
    limbs of the Trojans,
While from his inmost heart their king poured
    forth his petitions: 55
"Phœbus, compassionate ever of Troy's over-
    whelming disasters;
Thou who didst guide the hand and Dardanian
    arrow of Paris
'Gainst Achilles' frame, my pilot o'er many dark
    billows,
Breaking on boundless shores; my guide to Mas-
    sylian peoples,
Far remote; and to lands far fringed by the Lib-
    yan Syrtes,   60
Now that at last we are come to fugitive Italy's
    seacoast,
Let it suffice that the Fates of Troy thus far have
    pursued us.
Ye, too, well may be reconciled now to the Perga-
    mene nation,
Gods and goddesses all, whom Ilium e'er hath
    offended,
Or the great Dardan name. And thou, O priest-
    ess most holy,   65

Thou that foreknowest the future, O grant (and
    I ask for no kingdom
Promised me not by fate) that Latium harbor the
    Trojans,
Shelter their wandering gods and Teucria's trou-
    bled Penates;
Trivia, then, to thee and to Phœbus a temple of
    massive
Marble will I erect, and games shall be named for
    Apollo;   70
Thee, too, Sibyl benign, great shrines await in our
    kingdom;
For I will treasure thy oracles there, and the mys-
    tic arcana
Unto our race revealed; and chosen men to thy
    service
I will ordain. But, oh, write not upon leaves thy
    responses,
Lest, at the sport of the wind, they fly disturbed
    from their order;   75
Sing them thyself, I pray." Then, closing his
    lips, he is silent.
    Not submissive, however, as yet to Apollo, the
        fearful
Prophetess raves in the cavern, and still the great
    god from her bosom
Hopes to be able to drive; her frenzied lips the
    more sternly
Ruling, Apollo curbs and masters her furious
    spirit.   80
Now, of their own accord, the ponderous doors of
    the temple
Open their hundred mouths, and utter the word of
    the Sibyl.

" Hail to thee, finally done with the sea and its
    manifold perils !
Graver, however, of land remain. The Dardans
    shall enter
Into Lavinian realms ; dismiss this care from thy
    bosom, —   85
But they shall likewise repent of their coming,
    for battles, grim battles
Now I behold, and the Tiber all foaming with
    blood and with carnage !
Neither shall Simois fail thee, nor Xanthus, nor
    Doric encampments ;
Cradled already in Latium rises a second Achilles ;
Goddess-born, too, is he ; nor e'er will implacable
    Juno   90
Far from the Teucrians be ; while thou, as a sup-
    pliant beggar,
Where shalt thou wander not, among Italy's na-
    tions or cities ?
Sorely the Trojans shall suffer again from a for-
    eign alliance,
And from an alien bride.
Yield not thou to misfortunes, but go the more
    bravely to meet them,   95
Up to the limit thy Fates permit. The first way
    of safety,
What will surprise thee most, from a town of the
    Grecians will open."
  Thus from her hidden shrine the Sibyl of Cumæ
    replying,
Chanted her fearful enigmas, and thundered them
    forth from her cavern,
Darkly involving the truth ; such force, while she
    rages, Apollo   100

Uses to urge her on, and goads her wild spirit to
    frenzy.
Soon as her raving subsides, and her furious lips
    become silent,
Answers Æneas the hero: " O maiden, not one
    of my trials
Rises before my view as a startling or strange
    apparition ;
I have already imagined them all, and endured
    them in spirit ;   105
Only since here, we are told, are the gates of the
    monarch infernal,
Also the murky pool of the fountain of Acheron,
    be it
Mine to look once more on the face of my father
    belovéd ;
Show me the path to take, throw wide the terrible
    portals !
Him on my shoulders I hurried through flames
    and a thousand pursuing   110
Weapons, and bore him away unharmed from the
    midst of his foemen.
Long he companioned my way ; he shared all the
    perils of ocean ;
Patiently suffered with me all the threats of the
    sea and the heavens,
Weak as he was, and beyond an old man's lot or
    endurance.
Nay, it was he who implored and enjoined me to
    go to thy threshold   115
Seeking thy favor. I humbly entreat thee, kind
    maiden, to pity
Father and son, for pow'r unbounded is thine, and
    not vainly

Hecate set thee here to govern the groves of Aver-
    nus.

If, upon tuneful lyre and Thracian cithern rely-
    ing,

Orpheus was able to charm Eurydice's spirit from
    Hades,   120

If, by dying alternately, Pollux, redeeming his
    brother,

Trod and retrod the path so often, why call to re-
    membrance

Theseus or Hercules mighty? I, too, have a birth-
    right in Heaven."

   While he was praying thus, and holding the
    horns of the altar,

Thus did the Sibyl begin her reply: "O child of
    Immortals,   125

Trojan son of Anchises, descent to Avernus is
    easy;

Both by night and by day the gates of grim Pluto
    stand open;

But to retrace the step, to get back to the air and
    the sunlight,

This is labor and toil. A few have been able to
    do it,

Heirs of the gods, whom Jove hath graciously
    loved, or a quenchless   130

Valor restored to earth. The space intervening
    vast forests

Guard, and Cocytus surrounds with sunless and
    wandering waters.

Yet, if so deep the desire of thy heart, if so urgent
    thy longing

Twice on the Stygian wave to embark, if twice
    upon gloomy

Tartarus thou wouldst gaze, if this labor of mad-
    ness delight thee,   135

Hear what must first be done. There's a tree in
    the heart of a forest,

Hiding within its gloom a branch all golden in
    leafage,

Golden in stem, and held to be sacred to Stygian
    Juno.

This the whole wood surrounds, and buries in val-
    leys of shadow.

Yet, before any have leave to descend to the earth's
    dark abysses,   140

First he must ravish away from the tree her gol-
    den-haired children ;

This for her own delight hath fair Proserpina
    ordered

Brought to herself. The first no sooner is plucked,
    than a second

Branch of like metal appears, as golden of leaf as
    the other.

Search for it, therefore, with eyes uplifted, and,
    when thou hast found it,   145

Grasp it with reverent hand, for thee will it wil-
    lingly follow,

Needing no force, if the fates are calling thee;
    otherwise never

Shalt thou by strength or by toughness of iron be
    able to move it.

More than all this, the corse of a comrade of thine
    lieth lifeless, —

Thou, alas, knowing it not! — and pollutes the
    whole fleet by its presence,   150

While thou art questioning fate, and lingering
    here at our threshold.

Him, to his place of rest, first bear, and bury the
  body ;
Lead black sheep to the altar ; let this be thy first
  expiation ;
So shalt thou look, at last, on the Stygian groves,
  and the kingdom
Trackless to living feet." She spake, closed her
  lips, and was silent.   155
 Now, with steadfast eyes and sorrowful aspect,
  Æneas
Walks forth, leaving the cavern, and secretly
  weighs in his bosom
Fate's mysterious ways. By his side ever faithful
  Achates
Goes as companion, with step as reluctant, and
  equally anxious.
Many the thoughts they exchange with each other
  in wide ranging converse ; 160
Which of their friends could the prophetess speak
  of as lifeless ? What body
Waited for burial ? Then, as they came, they
  beheld on the sandy
Shore, bereft of life by a death he deserved not,
  Misenus ;
Yes, Misenus, Æolides, ever the foremost in rous-
  ing
Men to the fight with his bugle, and kindling the
  battle with music.   165
He the friend of great Hector had been, and to-
  gether with Hector
Rushed into battle, conspicuous both for his spear
  and his trumpet.
Then, after Hector had died by the sword of tri-
  umphant Achilles,

Unto Æneas, the Dardan, Misenus transferred his
    allegiance,
Bravest of heroes, himself, nor found a less noble
    commander.   170
But when it chanced that he deafened the sea with
    his echoing conch-shell,
When, with his trumpet, he challenged the gods to
    a contest of music,
Then, if the story be true, in the fury of envy had
    Triton
Caught him amid the rocks, and drowned him in
    foam-crested surges.
So, with loud lament, they all were mourning
    around him,   175
Chiefly devoted Æneas.   And then the commands
    of the Sibyl,
Weeping, but tarrying not, they haste to obey, and
    they labor
Gathering trees, and piling them high for a funeral
    altar.
Seeking the forest old, the majestic abode of wild
    creatures,
Resinous pines crash down ; the holm-oak rings
    with their axes ;   180
Ashen logs and straight-grained oaks are riven by
    wedges ;
Down from the hills they roll the trunks of huge
    mountain ash-trees.
Here, too, amid such toil, Æneas, as ever the
    leader,
Urges his comrades on, and is girded with tools
    like the others.
He with his own sad heart, however, is deeply com-
    muning,   185

Scanning the boundless wood, and at last gives
    voice to his longing :
"Now, if that golden bough should suddenly
    gleam on our vision,
Out of a forest so vast ! since all things the pro-
    phetess truly, —
Ah, as relates to thee, Misenus, — too truly hath
    spoken."
Scarce hath he uttered these words, when a pair of
    wild doves chance to flutter   190
Down from the sky overhead right under the eyes
    of Æneas,
Till on the verdant earth they rest. Then the
    greatest of heroes
Recognizes the birds of his Mother, and prays with
    rejoicing :
"Ah, if there be any path, may ye be my guides,
    through the heavens
Winging your way to the groves where the golden-
    leaved bough overshadows   195
Darkly the forest mould ; and do thou in my blind-
    ness be near me,
O my mother divine ! " So speaking, he halted
    his footsteps,
Watching what omen they bear, and whither their
    course may be tending.
Gleaning and feeding they flutter before, but with
    flight never longer
Than can be kept in view by the keen-eyed watch-
    ers who follow.   200
Now, when later they come to the pestilent gulf
    of Avernus,
Swiftly they rise aloft, and, through the clear at-
    mosphere gliding,

Deep in the two-fold tree sink down in their favo-
    rite covert,
Whence the contrasted hue of gold gleams out
    through the branches.
As in the cold of December the mistletoe, deep in
    the forest,   205
Nursed by an alien tree, is wont to grow green
    with new leafage,
While with a burgeon of sunshine it brightens the
    tapering tree-trunks ;
So from the dark holm-oak flashed a vision of
    foliage golden,
So in the gentle breeze the leaves of gold softly
    rustled.
Quickly Æneas hath seized it, and eagerly, spite
    of its clinging,   210
Plucks it, and bears it away to the shrine of the
    soothsaying Sibyl.
    Meanwhile, with no less devotion, the Teucrians
    mourn for Misenus,
Paying to thankless clay the last sad rites, by the
    seashore.
Rich with resinous pine, and big with hewn oaken
    timbers,
First they build a pyre, interweaving the sides with
    dark branches,   215
Also arranging in front thick rows of funereal
    cypress,
While they adorn it above with the glittering arms
    of Misenus.
Some, with lotions warm and caldrons hot from
    the embers,
Bathe the cold limbs of the dead, and anoint the
    inanimate body.

Wailings arise, and now, with tears, they are lay-
    ing the body   220
Down on the couch, over all disposing his gar-
    ments of purple,
Raiment remembered well. Then others draw
    nigh the great altar, —
Sorrowful service, — applying the torch, and avert-
    ing their faces
After the way of their fathers, and offerings burn
    in profusion, —
Frankincense, flesh of beasts, and jars of the oil
    of the olive.   225
After the ashes had sifted down and the flame had
    subsided,
Wine o'er the cinders they poured, and cooled the
    hot thirst of the embers,
While, in an urn of bronze, the gathered bones
    Corynæus
Covered, and thrice around his comrades passed
    with pure water,
Flinging a delicate spray from a branch of the
    fruit-bearing olive,   230
Purifying the men and pronouncing the last bene-
    diction.
But god-fearing Æneas a massive tomb hath
    erected,
Setting upon it the arms of the hero, his oar and
    his trumpet,
Under a cloud-capped hill, still called by Italians,
    Misenus,
So that his name lives on through the ages forever
    and ever.   235
    When this is finished he quickly obeys the com-
    mand of the Sibyl.

There was a bottomless pit, wide yawning with
    frightful abysses,
Jagged, and guarded by darkening waves and
    shadowy forests,
Over which none of the birds that fly had ever
    been able
Safely to wing their way, so deadly and dense
    exhalations   240
Rose from its murky throat to the lofty dome of
    the heavens ;
Wherefore this dismal lake had been named by
    the Grecians, Avernus.
Here hath the priestess at first ranged four black
    bullocks in order,
Then on the brow of each a libation of wine is
    outpouring,
And from between the horns, the hairs that are
    uppermost plucking,   245
These on the sacred fire she lays as the first expi-
    ation,
Hecate loudly invoking, who rules both in Hell
    and in Heaven.
Others draw knife to the throat, and catch the hot
    blood in their goblets ;
While Æneas himself a black-fleeced lamb with
    his sword-blade,
Unto the Mother of Furies and unto her powerful
    sister   250
Slays, and a barren cow, to thee, O Proserpina,
    offers.
Then to the Stygian king he consecrates altars at
    midnight,
Laying upon the flames the inward parts of the
    bullocks,

Firm and unbroken, and pouring rich oil on the
   hot blazing vitals.

But, as the first faint flush of morning foretokened
   the sunrise,   255

Rumbled the earth beneath, and a waving began
   in the topmost

Boughs of the forest, and hounds bayed loud in
   the darkness to herald

Hecate's advent. " Avaunt! Avaunt, ye profane,"
   cried the Sibyl;

" Far be your feet withdrawn; depart one and all
   from the forest!

But, do thou dare the way, thy sword pluck forth
   from the scabbard;   260

Now hadst thou needs be bold, now steadfast of
   heart, O Æneas!"

Speaking no more, she hath flung herself frenziedly into the cavern.

He, with resolute step, keeps pace with the stride
   of his escort.

   Gods, whose dominion is over the dead! and ye,
      voiceless shadows!

Chaos, and Phlegethon, too, ye realms far silent
   in darkness,   265

Sanction me now to reveal the things I have heard;
   let me open

Mysteries hid in the depths of the earth beneath
   her dark vapor.

   Under the shield of the silent night they went
      through the shadow,

Through the unpeopled abodes of Dis, and his
   ghostly dominions,

As by the treacherous light of the faithless moon,
   in a forest,   270

Travellers pass when Jove hath buried the heavens
    in shadow,
And dark night hath stolen the color from every
    object.
Hard by the mouth of Hell, where yawn the wide
    portals infernal,
Grief and avenging Care have fixed their slumber-
    less couches;
Here wan Sickness dwells, with wretched Age for
    a neighbor,   275
Sordid Penury, too, and Fear, and desperate Fam-
    ine;
Shapes that affright the eye; and Death and La-
    bor and Slumber,
Dull twin brother to Death, and the guilty Joys of
    the spirit.
Near to the opposite portal, lo! death-dealing
    War is abiding;
There are the iron cells of the Furies, and Dis-
    cord, in frenzy   280
Binding together her viperous tresses with blood-
    crimsoned fillets.
    Midway, a gloomy elm vast boughs and centuried
      branches
Giant-like stretches abroad, and there false dreams
    have their dwelling, —
So it is said, — and beneath all the leaves they are
    swarming and clinging.
There are the phantoms besides of a myriad mon-
    sters prodigious;   285
Centaurs are stalled in the entrance, with Scylla,
    half beast and half human,
Hundred-handed Briareus, too, and the Dragon of
    Lerna,

Horribly hissing; and, armed with breathings of
    flame, the Chimæra;
Gorgons, and Harpies dire, and Geryon's three-
    headed spectre.
Then, in sudden alarm, Æneas, unsheathing his
    dagger,   290
Flashes the naked blade in defiance of all who
    approach him;
And did his wiser guide not warn him that light,
    unsubstantial
Beings are flitting about in the shadowy semblance
    of bodies,
He would rush on, and in vain with steel strike
    shadows asunder.
    Hence is the way that leads to Tartarean Ache-
    ron's billows;   295
Here, aroil with slime, and with vortex vast, is a
    whirlpool,
Seething, and all its mud disgorging into Cocy-
    tus.
Guarding these waters and floods is a boatman,
    beheld with a shudder,
Charon, of terrible filth, whose great gray beard
    all neglected
Flows from his chin; his eyes out-standing like
    fiery torches,   300
Dingy the mantle and foul that hangs in a knot
    from his shoulders.
Poling his barge himself, he handles the sails un-
    assisted,
While in his dusky skiff he ferries the dead o'er
    the river;
Old, even now, but a god's old age is ruddy and
    rugged.

Hither a straggling crowd were all rushing down
    to the margin, —   305
Matrons and men, and the souls, discharged from
    life's duty, of heroes
Valiant of heart, and of boys, and unmarried girls,
    and of children
Laid on funeral pyres before the sad eyes of their
    parents,
Many as are the leaves that fall at the first cold of
    autumn
Far in the forest, or thick as the birds that from
    Ocean's deep waters   310
Gather in flight to land when icy Winter pursues
    them
Over the billows, and urges them on to a sunnier
    climate.
Standing there, then, they begged to be first in
    making the crossing;
Stretching out their hands to the further shore in
    entreaty;
But the inflexible ferryman, choosing now one,
    now another,   315
Drives the others away far back from the banks
    of the river.
Moved and amazed by the tumult, Æneas cries,
    "Tell me, O maiden,
What is the will of this multitude thronging the
    bank of the river?
What do these souls desire? Or say with what
    discrimination
These retire from the shore, while those are swept
    o'er the dark waters?"   320
Briefly the prophetess old replied to the question
    as follows: —

"Son of Anchises, assuredly sprung from the
    gods, thou art looking

Down on the Stygian lake, and the slumbering
    depths of Cocytus,

Taking an oath in whose name e'en the gods are
    afraid to be faithless.

All this throng thou beholdest are poor and unfu-
    neraled people ;   325

Yonder old ferryman, Charon ; those crossing the
    river, the buried ;

None may he bear across these dreadful shores and
    hoarse waters,

Till in their quiet graves their bodies are peace-
    fully sleeping.

Near to these banks for an hundred years they
    wander and hover,

Then are permitted once more to return to the
    coveted waters."   330

Paused the son of Anchises, and halted his hurry-
    ing footsteps,

Pondering deeply, and touched to the heart by their
    grievous condition.

Broken by grief and bereft of funereal honors,
    Leucaspis

There he beholds, and Orontes who captained the
    Lycian squadron,

Whom, as together they sailed from Troy o'er
    tempestuous billows,   335

Blasts from the south overwhelmed, and sunk both
    the ship and the sailors.

    Hastening eagerly forward, behold Palinurus,
    the pilot !

Who, but now, while he watched the stars on the
    voyage from Carthage,

Fell from the lofty stern and was lost in the midst
    of the billows.

When through the darkness he recognized dimly
    the sorrowful features,   340

Thus he was first to speak. "What one of the
    gods, Palinurus,

Snatched thee away from our ship, and buried thee
    deep in the ocean?

Quick! thy reply, for my faith, in this response
    only, Apollo —

Never before found false — hath betrayed; for he
    sang that from ocean

Thou shouldst receive no harm; and he sang that
    Ausonia's borders   345

Thou shouldst attain. Alas! is it thus he redeem-
    eth his promise?"

He, however, replied; "O son of Anchises, nor
    Phœbus

Thee hath deceived, nor me hath a god over-
    whelmed in the ocean;

For as I headlong fell, I chanced to drag with me
    the tiller

Forcibly wrenched away, to which, as its author-
    ized keeper,   350

Firmly I clung, and directed our course; wild
    waves, be my witness,

None so great fear for myself then seized me, as
    fear for thy vessel,

Lest, of her rudder bereft, and suddenly robbed
    of her pilot,

She should despair in the midst of so rude and
    tempestuous surges.

Over the boundless sea, three dark stormy nights
    through the water   355

Violent winds from the south impelled me.   The
    fourth day was dawning
When from the top of a wave, high tossing, I
    faintly discovered
Italy, toward whose shores I wearily swam, and
    had gained them,
Had not a barbarous people, in vain expectation
    of plunder,
Fallen upon me with swords, as, heavy with brine-
    dripping garments,   360
Clutching with fingers bent, I grappled the sharp
    rocky ledges.
Me doth the flood now hold, and winds roll about
    on the seashore.
But, by the pleasant light, by heaven's sweet air,
    I implore thee,
By thy filial love, by the promise of rising Iulus,
Rescue me from these waves, thou hero unvan-
    quished, by sprinkling   365
Earth on my bones, — thou canst, by searching
    the port of Velinum ;
Or, if there be any way, if thy mother divine any
    guidance
Giveth (for not, I believe, without the approval of
    Heaven
Thou art attempting to pass these floods and Sty-
    gian waters),
Give a poor wretch thine hand, and carry me, too,
    o'er the billows,   370
So that, at least in death, I may peacefully rest
    from my labors."
Such were the words he spake, and thus did the
    prophetess answer :
" Whence this longing of thine, so impious, O
    Palinurus ?

Shalt thou, unburied, behold the Stygian wave, or
    the cruel
River of Furies, or tread unbidden the marge of
    the river ?   375
Banish the hope that the Fates of the gods can be
    changed by entreaty.
None the less cherish these words to solace thy
    bitter misfortunes.
Far and wide through their cities pursued by the
    portents of Heaven,
They that live near to thy bones shall pay them
    the rites of atonement ;
They shall both build thee a tomb, and bear to
    the tomb their oblations,   380
So that the place shall preserve thy name, Palinu-
    rus, forever."
Then by these words are his cares removed ; from
    the sorrowful spirit
Slowly is grief dispelled ; in the name-honored
    land he rejoices.
So they continue their journey begun, and draw
    nigh to the river.
Now as the Stygian ferryman looked from the
    wave, and perceived them   385
Threading the silent wood, and shoreward bend-
    ing their footsteps,
Straightway attacking with words, he angrily chal-
    lenged their coming : —
" Thou, whoever thou art, who bravest our stream
    with thy weapons,
Speak ! Why comest thou ? Halt ! Reply, but
    advance at thy peril.
This is the region of shades, of sleep, and of
    slumberous midnight.   390

Living bodies to bear in our Stygian craft is for-
    bidden.

When I received on the lake Alcides himself at
    his coming,

It was no joy to me; nor Pirithous pleased me, nor
    Theseus,

Though they were sprung from the gods and were
    also by mortals unvanquished.

That one seized with his hands the warder of Hell,
    and he dragged him   395

Forth from the very throne of the King, enchained
    and affrighted;

These attempted to force the Queen from the
    chamber of Pluto."

Briefly to him replied the Amphrysian Sibyl as
    follows: —

" No such insidious plots are here — thy fear is
    ungrounded;

Nor do our arms bring force. Lo, still in his den
    your gigantic   400

Warder may bark his fill, and frighten pale
    shadows forever;

Still by her uncle's door may chaste Proserpina
    linger.

Trojan Æneas, renowned alike for his faith and
    his valor,

Through the profoundest shades of Erebus goes to
    his father.

If thou art not constrained by so noble a proof of
    devotion,   405

Yet this branch " — and she showed him the
    branch that lay hid in her bosom —

" Thou mayest know." His heart then sinks from
    its tumult of passion;

Speaking no more, and awed by the mystical gift
    of the fateful
Branch not seen before for many a year, the dull
    colored
Vessel he turned about, and pushed in close into
    the margin.   410
Then, the unbodied shades, that on the long
    benches were huddled,
Routing, he cleared the boat, at the same time into
    its hollow
Taking unwieldy Æneas, beneath whose weight the
    stitched shallop
Groaned, and its leaky sides drank deep of the
    trickling water.
Over the stream at last, unharmed, both Sibyl and
    hero   415
Deep in a dismal swamp, 'mid sea-green sedges he
    landed.
Cerberus, stretching his monstrous bulk in an op-
    posite cavern,
Makes these regions resound with the noise of his
·   three-throated howling.
Now, as she sees his necks upbristling with ser-
    pents, the seeress
Flings him a sop imbrued with honey and somno-
    lent juices.   420
He, with hunger mad, his three throats widely dis-
    tending,
Catches it ere it falls, and, relaxing his powerful
    haunches,
Prone on the earth lies huge along the whole length
    of the cavern.
Seizing the pass, while its keeper is buried in
    slumber, Æneas

Swiftly withdraws from the brink of the river
 noue ever recrosses.   425
 Presently cries are heard, and the sound of a
  great lamentation,
And, at the outer gate, the wailing spirits of chil-
 dren,
Babes unsharing in life's delight, and torn from
 the bosom,
Whom a dark day bore away, and plunged into
 Death's bitter waters.
Next abide those condemned to death upon false
 accusation ;   430
Nor are these places assigned without formal allot-
 ment of judges ;
Minos, presiding, impanels a jury, assembling a
 silent
Council of ghosts, and investigates fully their lives
 and transgressions.
Stations next these are reserved for the sorrowing
 spirits, who guiltless,
By their own hands found death, and hurled their
 souls into darkness,   435
Loathing the light. But, ah! how willingly now
 would they suffer
Hunger and bitter toil, if restored to the land of
 the living!
Heaven forbids, and the mournful ooze of desolate marshes
Holds, and the Styx restrains, nine times enfolded
 around them.
Near by, also, are shown the Plains of Lamentation, —   440
Such is the name they bear, — extending far over
 the valley.

Here lone pathways hide, and groves of myrtle
    o'ershadow
Those whom pitiless love hath wasted with cruel
    repining;
Not in death itself are they freed from the thral-
    dom of passion.
Phædra and Procris he saw, and there he saw sad
    Eryphyle,   445
Showing the wounds received from her cruel son;
    and Evadne,
Pasiphae, also; with whom Laodamia went as com-
    panion;
Cæneus, too, now changed once more from a man
    to a maiden,
Dowered again by fate with the vanished grace of
    her girlhood;
Compassed about by whom, her bosom still bleed-
    ing, Phœnician   450
Dido came wandering on in the boundless wood,
    and the Trojan
Hero, soon as he stood by her side and distin-
    guished her shadowed
Form, as one who sees, or thinks he hath seen, in
    the early
Dawn of the month, amid clouds, a glimmer of
    silvery moonlight,
Burst into tears, and spoke with tenderest words
    of affection: 455
" Then were the tidings true that reached me, un-
    fortunate Dido?
' Dido is dead; by the sword she hath ended her
    life and her trouble.'
Ah, and have I been the cause of thy death? I
    swear by the heavens,

By the great gods above, by whatsoe'er oath Hell
    regardeth,
Not of mine own desire, O Queen, did I loose
    from thy harbor;   460
But the commands of the gods, that are driving
    me now through these shadows,
Through this wilderness tangle of thorn and mid-
    night darkness,
By their own power constrained; nor could I at all
    have imagined
That I should bring thee by going so grievous a
    burden of sorrow.
Stay thine impatient feet! withdraw thyself not
    from our presence.   465
Whom dost thou flee? These words are the last
    fate grants us forever."
Thus did Æneas endeavor to soothe her implaca-
    ble spirit,
And to bring tears to the eyes where fierce indig-
    nation was burning.
She, with averted face, remained looking fixedly
    downward,
Changed in expression no more, as Æneas began
    to entreat her,   470
Than if hard flint she stood, or a rock on the
    mount of Marpessa.
Finally, breaking away, unrelenting, she hurries
    for refuge
Into the shadowy grove, and there her first lover,
    Sychæus,
Comforts her every care, and answers her heart's
    deepest longing.
Nevertheless, dismayed by her undeserved anguish,
    Æneas   475

Follows her far on her way with tears of compassion and sorrow.

Thence his allotted way he toils; and now they are
 gaining

Those most distant fields reserved for illustrious
 heroes.

Tydeus meets him here, and Parthenopæus, distinguished

Highly in war; here, too, appears the pale shade
 of Adrastus;   480

Here, lamented on earth, the Dardanians fallen in
 battle,

Whom in a long array, beholding, he groaned in
 his spirit.

Glaucus he recognized there, Thersilochus also,
 and Medon,

Three of Antenor's line, Polyphætes, the servant
 of Ceres,

Also Idæus, who still retained both his car and his
 armor.   485

Frequent to right and left the spirits come thronging about him,

Nor does one look suffice; they are ever delighted
 to linger,

Eager to walk by his side, and question the cause
 of his coming.

Ah! but the chiefs of the Greeks, and Agamemnon's battalions,

When they behold the man and his glittering arms
 through the shadows,   490

Tremble with deadly fear; and some turn their
 backs in confusion,

Or, as of yore, retreat to their ships; others raise
 unavailing

Cries; their voices die on lips wide parted, but
    silent.
Here Deiphobus, too, son of Priam, he sees, with
    his body
Wounded from head to foot, his features all cru-
    elly mangled;   495
Marred are his face and his hands; his temples are
    robbed of their beauty;
Shorn are his ears, and his nose by a hideous cut
    is disfigured.
Hardly he knew him at all, as he tremblingly cov-
    ered his frightful
Wounds, yet he instantly spoke in his well-known
    voice to the hero: —
" Valiant and mighty Deiphobus, sprung from the
    proud blood of Teucer,   500
Who hath desired to inflict so cruel a punishment
    on thee?
Who hath been suffered to injure thee thus?   It
    was rumored among us
During that fatal night, that exhausted by killing
    so many,
Thou hadst fallen at last on a mound of Pelasgian
    corpses.
Then on the Rhœtian shore, by a cenotaph raised
    in thine honor,   505
Taking my stand, I called three times and aloud
    on thy spirit;
Now thy name and thine arms are guarding the
    place; thee, my comrade,
Vainly I sought, ere departing, to lay in the soil
    of thy country."
Answered the son of Priam: " My friend, thou
    hast nothing neglected;

Thou hast done all for Deiphobus, all for the spirit
    departed.   510
Naught but my fate and the murderous crime of
    the Spartan hath plunged me
Into these ills; it is she that hath left me these
    marks of remembrance;
For, how that fatal night we passed in ill-founded
    rejoicing,
Well dost thou know, too well to need any word
    of reminder.
Soon as the fatal horse leaped over our towering
    ramparts,   515
Pregnant with steel, and filled with a legion of
    soldiers in armor,
She, on pretence of a festival, marshalled the
    Phrygian matrons,
Dancing with Bacchanal songs, herself in the midst
    with a flaming
Torch, and she called to the Greeks from the lof-
    tiest point of the fortress.
Me, with care forespent, and buried in sleep, my
    ill omened   520
Chamber was sheltering then; and a deep and
    delectable slumber,
Likest the stupor of death, was weighing me down
    as I lay there.
Meanwhile my excellent wife had removed all my
    arms from the palace,
Even my faithful sword she had stolen from under
    my pillow;
Into the palace she called Menelaus; my door she
    threw open,   525
Hoping, forsooth, to bestow a most precious re-
    ward on her lover,

Ay! and that thus might be purged all the sin
    and the shame of her lifetime.
Why do I linger? They burst my door; one com-
    rade is added,
Even that father of crime, Ulysses. Ye gods!
    to the Grecians
Recompense grant in kind, if I with clean lips de-
    mand vengeance!   530
But, in return, say, now, what chances have
    brought thee, still living,
Into this place? Dost come by ocean wanderings
    driven;
Or by the gods' decree? or what is the fortune
    constrains thee
Saddened and sunless abodes and realms of confu-
    sion to visit?"
  While they exchanged these words, already Au-
    rora had traversed,   535
High in her rosy car, the meridian line of the
    heavens.
All their allotted time might perhaps have been
    spent in this manner,
But their companion gave warning, and briefly the
    Sibyl admonished: —
"Night rushes on, O Æneas; we squander our
    moments in weeping;
This is the place where the path divides into oppo-
    site courses;   540
One on the right to the city of Pluto the mighty
    extending; —
We to Elysium thus; — but that on the left retri-
    bution
Brings to the damned, and sends them down to
    regions infernal."

Answered Deiphobus, " Nay, great priestess, give
    over thine anger,
I will depart, I will fill the roll, and return to the
    shadows :   545
Onward, our Glory, on ! Improve thine happier
    fortunes ! "
So much only he spake, and speaking turned back-
    ward his footsteps.
   Quickly Æneas looks back, and sees a broad
    city extending
Under a cliff to the left, surrounded by triplicate
    bulwarks.
Round it the swift flowing stream of Tartarean
    Phlegethon rushes,   550
Surging with flames of fire, and roaring through
    rock-laden channel.
Huge was the gate in front, with impregnable
    adamant columns,
So that no might of man, nor e'en the battalions
    of Heaven
Warring against it prevail ; high looms the grim
    fortress of iron ;
While Tisiphone, girt with her blood-dripping
    mantle, is crouching,   555
Guarding the entrance by night and by day with
    no respite of slumber.
Hence from afar deep groans were heard, and the
    echo of cruel
Scourging, and dragging of chains, and the sound
    of the clanking of iron.
Halted Æneas, and stood dismayed by the noise,
    and bewildered.
" What are these forms of crime ? Speak boldly,
    O maiden, and answer.   560

What are the pains they bear? Why rises this
    wailing to heaven?"
Thus, then, the priestess replied: "O glorious
    chief of the Trojans,
No pure spirit is suffered to pass that threshold
    infernal;
But, when great Hecate placed the Avernian
    grove in my keeping,
She, herself, showed me all Hell, and taught me
    the judgments of Heaven.   565
  Over these stern domains, Rhadamanthus, the
    Cretan, presiding,
Tortures hypocrisy true, and forces the false to
    confession
Even of crime committed on earth, whose late ex-
    piation
Any deferred until death, exulting in futile decep-
    tion.
Armed with her scourges, avenging Tisiphone
    lashes the guilty,   570
Ceaselessly taunting their woe, her left hand lift-
    ing her cruel
Serpents on high, and she calls her pitiless army
    of sisters.
Then, with a creaking of harsh, grating hinges,
    the terrible portals
Open before them at last.   Dost see what manner
    of warden
Sits in the outer porch, what a shape is on guard
    at the threshold?   575
Hydra, more cruel and huge, her fifty dark mouths
    gaping open,
Watches the gate within; then Tartarus, yawning
    before you,

Plunges as far again sheer down into regions of
    darkness
As to our upward gaze high tower the crests of
    Olympus.
Here do the first-born children of Earth, her off-
    spring Titanic,   580
Hurled by the thunder down, still writhe in its
    deepest abysses.
Here, too, I saw the Aloïdan twins, gigantic of
    stature,
Who with their hands essayed to rend the vast
    arch of the heavens,
And to thrust Jupiter down from his throne of
    celestial dominion.
There, too, I witnessed the fearful atonement Sal-
    moneus rendered,   585
Daring to imitate Jupiter's fire, and Olympian
    thunder,
Borne in a four-horse car, and brandishing torches,
    he proudly
Passed through the tribes of Greece, and the prin-
    cipal city of Elis.
Madman! to claim for himself the honor due only
    to Heaven,
Counterfeiting with brass and the horny hoofs of
    his horses   590
Cloud, and tempest, and hail, and the matchless
    voice of the thunder!
But, from an angry sky, one bolt the omnipotent
    Father
Hurling, — not firebrands, he, nor flaring and
    smouldering torches, —
Dashed him headlong down by the awful breath
    of his lightning.

Tityos, son of all-mothering earth, could be recog-
    nized also,   595
Stretched on the ground, his frame o'er nine whole
    acres extending,
While, with its curving beak, a ravenous vulture
    forever
Tearing his undying liver and vitals prolific of tor-
    ment,
Worries about for its food, and under his ribs'
    lofty arches
Ever abides, and allows no rest to the burgeoning
    fibres.   600
Why of the Lapithæ speak, of Pirithous, or of
    Ixion,
Whom a dark rock overhangs, ever slipping, and
    trembling, and seeming
Certain to fall; the frames of grand and luxuri-
    ous couches
Glitter with gold, and feasts that a monarch might
    envy are standing
Full in their view; but the chief of the Furies,
    couching beside them,   605
Instantly leaps to her feet if they stretch forth
    their hands to the tables,
Beating them back with her torch, and thundering
    curses upon them.
Here, whoever on earth hath been guilty of hating
    a brother,
Whoso hath beaten a parent, or broken faith with
    a client,   ·
All who have selfishly clung to treasure unearthed
    by good fortune,   610
Setting apart no share for their friends — and this
    throng is the greatest —

All for adultery slain, and all who have joined in
    sedition,
Daring to break their oaths and plighted vows of
    allegiance;
All, here imprisoned, await their reward. Seek
    not to discover
What that punishment is, or what manner of doom
    hath o'erwhelmed them.   615
Some a huge rock must roll, or, immovably fas-
    tened, are hanging
Stretched by the spokes of wheels; there sits, and
    shall sit through the ages,
Heart-broken Theseus, while Phlegyas mournfully
    · cries through the shadows,
Testifying aloud, and admonishing all who will
    listen,
' Learn from my fate to be just, and hold not the
    gods in derision.'   620
This one hath bartered his country for gold, and
    a powerful tyrant
Placed on the throne, and laws for a price hath
    ordained and abolished;
This with unholy desire hath dishonored the name
    of a daughter;
All have dared some infamous crime, and daring,
    achieved it.
Not, if an hundred tongues were mine, if mine
    were an hundred   625
Mouths, and an iron voice, could I tell all the
    forms of transgression,
Or all the names rehearse of the retributions they
    suffer."
    Soon as the reverend priestess of Phœbus had
        ended her story,

"Speed on your way," she cried ; "now finish the
 course undertaken.
Hasten we onward! The walls wrought out in
 the forge of the Cyclops   630
Now I behold, and the gate in the arching rock
 that confronts us,
Where we are now required to surrender the gift
 we are bearing."
Silently, then, pressing forward together through
 shadowy pathways,
Swiftly they cover the space that remains, and
 draw nigh to the portal.
Quickly Æneas approaches the entrance, and over
 his body   635
Sprinkles pure water, and fastens the branch to
 the lintel before him.
    Finally, when this was done, and the rites of
 the goddess completed,
Into glad places they come, and delectable meadows, embosomed
Deep in delightful groves, the blessed abode of the
 righteous.
Here a sublimer air over-mantles the valleys with
 purple ;   640
Here their own stars they know, and their own
 sun shineth above them.
Some, in grassy courts, are training their disci-
 plined bodies,
Or, on the yellow sand, are contending in friendly
 encounter ;
Others are treading a dance, and marking the
 measure with carols ;
Nor does the Thracian bard, apparelled in long
 flowing garments,   645

Fail to awake from his lyre the varying notes of
the octave,
Striking them now with his fingers, and now with
an ivory plectrum.
Here is the ancient line of Teucer's illustrious
children,
Heroes noble of soul, and nurtured in happier
ages:
Ilus, Assaracus also, and Dardanus, Ilium's
founder.   650
Yonder the arms and the empty cars of the heroes
delight him;
Spears stand fixed in the earth, and, ranging at
large and untethered,
Horses are grazing the plain. All the fondness
for car and for armor
Ever confessed in life, their delight in the care of
their shining
Steeds, abides unchanged long after the body is
buried.   655
Others to right and left along the bright sward are
discovered
Feasting, and chanting hymns of glad thanksgiv-
ing in chorus,
Deep in a fragrant grove of laurel, from whence
to the valley
Rolls the abundant tide of Eridanus down through
the forest.
Here are the heroes who fell while fighting the
wars of their country,   660
Here are the holy priests whose lives upon earth
were unsullied,
Here the poets divine, who sang as inspired by
Apollo, —

All who have dignified life by the arts they have
    won by invention,
All who have worthily earned the lasting regard
    of their fellows,
All these, having their brows encircled with snow-
    white fillets,   665
Scattered in various groups, the Sibyl addresses as
    follows —
Chiefly Musæus, for him the most numerous band
    of companions
Gather about and revere, as he stands head and
    shoulders above them : —
" Tell us, ye fortunate souls, and thou most illus-
    trious poet,
Where is the region, and where the place that is
    holding Anchises ?   670
For, for his sake are we come, and have crossed
    the great river of Darkness."
Thereupon, briefly the hero replied to the ques-
    tioning Sibyl : —
"None hath a changeless abode ; we dwell in the
    shadowy forests,
Couch by the banks of streams, and wander
    through rill-freshened meadows ;
Yet if your hearts are so eagerly bent on fulfilling
    your mission,   675
Traverse this ridge, and soon I will set a smooth
    pathway before you."
Speaking, and taking the lead, he showed them, far
    down in the valley,
Sunlighted plains, and then they left the tall hill-
    tops behind them.
    But, in the midst of the green and hill-sheltered
    valley, Anchises

Chanced to be fondly reviewing the spirits impris-
    oned, and destined   680
Soon to the light of earth. Yes! there he stood
    reckoning over
All the long roll of his line, and all his belovéd
    descendants,
Reading the fortune and fate, and the conduct and
    wars of the heroes.
When he discovers Æneas approaching across the
    green meadow,
Eagerly both his arms are opened wide to receive
    him;   685
Wet are his cheeks with tears, and his lips break
    forth in rejoicing : —
" Comest thou, then, at last, and thy long-trusted
    love for thy father,
Hath it the hard way won? Am I suffered to
    gaze on thy features,
O my son; may we speak in the voices of old to
    each other ?
This I kept ever in mind, for this I was trusting
    the future,   690
Counting the lingering days; nor hath my heart's
    longing deceived me.
Borne over how many lands, and o'er what ex-
    panses of ocean,
Thee I receive, and by perils how great hath my
    son been encompassed!
How have I feared lest harm should befall thee in
    Libya's kingdom ! "
He, however, " O father, thine image, thy sorrow-
    ful image,   695
Fronting me often, constrained to continue my
    course to thy dwelling;

Moored is our fleet in the Tuscan sea. O give
    me, my father,
Give me thy hand to grasp; forbid thou me not to
    embrace thee!'"
Wet were his cheeks with tears, while thus he
    stood earnestly pleading;
Thrice he attempted to throw his arms 'round the
    neck of his father,   700
Thrice, unavailingly clasped, the image denied his
    embraces
Like the light kiss of the wind, still more like a
    dream in its swiftness.
    Meanwhile Æneas perceives a lonely grove in a
    distant
Part of the valley, and hears the whispering leaves
    of a forest,
Also peaceful abodes on the shore of the river of
    Lethe.   705
Hovering round about were peoples and tribes
    without number;
And, as in meadows where bees, in the cloudless
    sunshine of summer,
Cluster on varied flowers, and swarm about snow-
    white lilies,
So the whole plain is filled with the murmur of
    shadowy legions.
Dazed by so wondrous a sight, and knowing not
    what it portended,   710
Straightway, Æneas inquired the name of the far
    distant river,
Who were the men that were thronging its banks
    in so mighty a concourse.
Father Anchises replied: "The souls to whom
    fate hath appointed

Reincarnation are there, on the shore of the river
    of Lethe,
Endless release from care, and eternal oblivion
    quaffing.   715
These have I long desired to marshal in order
    before thee,
Naming thee all their names, and rehearsing our
    line of descendants,
So that in Italy won, thy joy and mine own may
    be greater."
" Must we, my father, believe that hence to the air
    and the daylight
Some of these souls will arise, and return into
    burdensome bodies ?   720
What so dread desire have sorrowful spirits for
    living ? "
" Surely, my son, I will answer, and leave thee no
    longer in darkness,"
Father Anchises replies, and discusses each ques-
    tion in order.
" In the beginning the air, and the earth, and the
    waters of ocean,
Also the moon's bright orb, the sun, and the great
    constellations,   725
Thrilled with an indwelling soul ; and a spirit, per-
    vading each atom,
Stirred the whole mass, and informed each part of
    the boundless creation :
Whence the race of men, and beasts, and birds
    was engendered, —
Yea, and the monsters that breed 'neath the mar-
    ble plain of the ocean.
Theirs is the vigor of fire, and celestial the source
    of their being,   730

Save as inimical bodies embarrass their freedom,
    and earth-born
Frames and corruptible members have deadened
    the fire of the spirit.
Hence are their fears and hopes, their griefs and
    their joys; and, in darkness,
Prisoned in sightless clay, they attain not the
    heavenly vision:
Nay, when the last faint glimmer of life shall have
    gone from the body,   735
Not even then shall all ills, nor all traces of carnal
    corruption,
Leave the unhappy soul; and it must be that
    manifold evils,
Slowly and deeply acquired, are ingrained in a
    marvellous manner.
Therefore by pain are they purged, and penance
    for former transgression
Pay to the uttermost; some, suspended, are spread
    to the fleeting   740
Winds; from others the stain of sin is washed by
    a whirling
Torrent of water away, or the spirit is chastened
    by burning;
Each his own chastisement bears; thence unto
    Elysium's freedom
We are dismissed, and we few in the fields of the
    blest are abiding
Till, when our cycle be ended, a day in the far
    distant future   745
Purge from the purified soul the last lingering ves-
    tige of evil,
Leaving a deathless flame of pure uncontaminate
    spirit.

After these souls have completed a full millennial
    circle,
God calls them all in a numberless band to the
    river of Lethe,
That, as the future dawns, the past may be wholly
    forgotten,   750
And that again may be born a desire for the life
    of the body ”
    Silent Anchises became, then guided his son and
    the Sibyl
Through the gathering throng to the midst of the
    murmuring concourse.
Then he selected a mound from whence to sur-
    vey the long column
Threading the distant plain, and study the faces
    approaching.   755
“ Come, now, let me unfold in words what glory
    the future
Holds for the Dardan race, what descendants in
    Italy wait thee,
Souls of illustrious heroes predestined thy name
    to inherit;
Listen, and I will reveal thy fate and the fate of
    thy people.
Seest thou yonder youth, who leans on an ironless
    spear-shaft ?   760
Fate hath assigned him the earliest place in the
    light; he shall soonest
Rise to the air above, old Troy with new Italy
    blending, —
Silvius, Alban the name, the latest born of thy
    children,
Whom in the years of thine age a Lavinian wife
    shall have borne thee ;

Child of the forest he, a king, with kings for de-
    scendants,   ₇₆₅
Whence o'er the long white city our line shall
    inherit dominion.
Next after him is that Procas, the pride of the
    Ilian nation,
Capys, and Numitor, too, and, reviving thy name
    and thy glory,
Silvius, surnamed Æneas, as famous for faith as
    for fighting,
If he shall ever attain his rightful dominion in
    Alba.   ₇₇₀
Ah! what youths they are! behold, what a vision
    of valor!
Proudly they lift their brows with civic oak over-
    shadowed!
These shall establish Nomentum, Fidena, and
    Gabii, for thee;
Those shall set on the hills the crown of Collatia's
    castles;
Castrum Inui, too, Pometia, Bola, and Cora;   ₇₇₅
Lands that are now unnamed shall bear these
    names in the future.
Ay! and the son of Mars shall forever be named
    with his grandsire;
Romulus, he who shall call Assaracan Ilia mother:
Seest thou how twin plumes stand forth as a crest
    from his helmet?
How the great Father hath set his own seal of
    divinity on him?   ₇₈₀
Lo, my son, thine illustrious Rome shall, under
    his sceptre,
Measure her empire with earth, and measure her
    valor with Heaven!

She, for herself and alone, seven hills shall sur‑
round with her ramparts,

Blest in her brood of men : as the Berecynthian
mother,

Crowned with her turrets, is borne in her car
through Phrygian cities, 785

Glad in the birth of gods, and embracing an hun‑
dred descendants,

Habitants all of the sky, all dwelling on lofty
Olympus.

Hitherward, now, concentre thy gaze ; look forth
on this nation ;

These, thy Romans, behold ! Lo, Cæsar and all
the Iulian

Line, predestined to rise to the infinite spaces of
heaven. 790

This, yea, this is the man, so often foretold thee in
promise,

Cæsar Augustus, descended from God, who again
shall a golden

Age in Latium found, in fields once governed by
Saturn.

Further than India's hordes, or the Garymantian
peoples,

He shall extend his reign ; there 's a land beyond
all of our planets, 795

'Yond the far track of the year and the sun, where
sky-bearing Atlas

Turns on his shoulders the firmament studded with
bright constellations ;

Yea, even now, at his coming foreshadowed by
omens from Heaven,

Shudder the Caspian realms, and the barbarous
Scythian kingdoms,

While the disquieted harbors of sevenfold Nile
    are affrighted!   800
Verily, neither Alcides e'er traversed so much of
    this planet,
Though he hath slaughtered the brazen-hoofed stag,
    and secured Erymanthus
Peace in his forest glades, though his bow hath
    made Lerna to tremble ;
Nor, who triumphantly guideth his coursers with
    vine-wreathéd bridle,
Bacchus, down-driving his tigers from Nysa's pre-
    cipitous mountains.   805
And do we hesitate still to broaden our prestige
    by valor ?
Or shall we yield to fear, and withdraw from Au-
    sonia's borders !
Ah, but who yonder is he, distinguished by
    branches of olive,
Sacred insignia bearing ? The locks and gray
    beard of the Roman
King I recognize there, who first shall establish a
    city   810
Founded in law ; he shall rise from the poor, nar-
    row acres of Cumæ
Unto an empire vast.   Then quickly shall come to
    succeed him
Tullus, predestined to break the repose of his
    country, and rally
Slumbering heroes, and troops unacquainted with
    conquest, to battle.
Next after him, behold vainglorious Ancus advan-
    cing,   815
Already, even now, too dependent on popular
    favor.

Seest thou, too, the Tarquinian kings, and the
    proud Roman spirit
Breathing in Brutus, th' avenger? behold ye the
    fasces recovered?
Consular power he first shall assume, and the ter-
    rible axes;
And, in fair Liberty's name, this father shall sen-
    tence his children   820
Unto the pains of death for conspiring against the
    Republic.
Ill-fated hero! However his deeds may be judged
    in the future,
Love for his country and boundless ambition for
    glory shall conquer!
Nay, but the Decii see, and the Drusi beyond, and
    Torquatus,
Pitiless with his axe, and Camillus restoring the
    standards.   825
Those, however, whose arms thou seest are equal
    in splendor,
Spirits harmonious now, and as long as the dark-
    ness constrains them,
How great a war, alas, shall they wage with each
    other, if ever
They shall attain to the light of life; what battle,
    what carnage!
Down from the Alpine heights and the walls of
    Monœcus, the father   830
Rushes to meet the son arrayed with Eastern bat-
    talions.
Suffer ye not, my lads, your souls to grow used to
    such conflicts;
Turn not your stalwart might against the life of
    your country!

And do thou first forbear, who tracest thy line to
    Olympus.
Fling from thy hand the spear, thou blood of my
    blood!   835
That one, renowned for the Greeks he hath slain,
    shall drive his triumphant
Car to the Capitol's height, when the city of Cor-
    inth is conquered;
That one shall Argos destroy, and Agamemnon's
    Mycenæ,
Capturing Perseus himself, the descendant of war-
    like Achilles,
Venging the sires of Troy, and the shrine of dis-
    honored Minerva.   840
Who can great Cato forget, or pass thee, O Cos-
    sus, in silence?
Who the two Gracchi, or Scipios twain, twin
    lightnings of battle,
Libya's scourge, or Fabricius, poverty crowning
    with honor?
Or who would name thee not, as thou sowest thy
    furrow, Serranus?
Whither, ye Fabii, bear ye the wearied?   That
    Maximus art thou   845
Who dost alone reëstablish our prestige in war by
    delaying.
  Others may fashion the breathing bronze with
    more delicate fingers;
Doubtless they also will summon more lifelike
    features from marble;
They shall more cunningly plead at the bar; and
    the mazes of heaven
Draw to the scale, and determine the march of the
    swift constellations;   850

Thine be the care, O Rome, to subdue the whole
    world to thine empire ;

These be the arts for thee, the order of peace to
    establish,

Them that are vanquished to spare, and them that
    are haughty to humble ! ''

Thus spake Father Anchises, and thus, as they
    marvel, continued : —

'' See how Marcellus advances, adorned with rich
    trophies of conquest !   855

How as a victor he comes, surpassing all heroes in
    glory !

Knightly defender of Rome, he shall save her
    from deadliest peril,

Crushing the armies of Carthage, and quelling the
    Gallic rebellion,

Offering trophies thrice in the temple of Father
    Quirinus.''

Then did Æneas exclaim, — for he saw, by the
    side of Marcellus,   860

Wondrous in beauty, a youth, arrayed in glitter-
    ing armor,

Yet with joyless brow, sad eyes, and sorrowful
    features : —

'' Who, my father, is he, who follows yon hero so
    closely ?

Is he his son, or one of his glorious line of de-
    scendants ?

Round him what comrades are surging ! Himself,
    how inspiring a presence !   865

Yet is dark night brooding over his head with the
    shadow of sorrow.''

Then, with a burst of tears, doth Father Anchises
    make answer : —

"Ah! seek not, my son, to learn the deep grief of
    thy people;
Fate shall vouchsafe to the world but a glimpse of
    his glory, nor suffer
Earth to detain him long.   Too great in your eyes
    would the Roman   870
Nation appear, ye gods, were gifts such as these to
    be lasting!
What lamentation of men shall arise from yon
    plain to the mighty
City of Mars! and what funeral rites shalt thou
    witness,
While by his new-made grave thou shalt mourn-
    fully ripple, O Tiber!
Neither shall ever a son of the Ilian line raise the
    Latin   875
Fathers to hope so high, nor e'er shall the land of
    the Roman
Glory so proudly again in any one of her chil-
    dren.
Ah, what devotion, what freshness of faith, and,
    unconquered in battle,
What a right arm were his!   There were none
    who could safely withstand him,
Whether with arms he should march on foot to
    encounter his foemen,   880
Or should he plunge the spur in the flank of his
    foam-dappled charger.
Ah! thou child of our tears, if thou breakest
    from fate's bitter bondage,
Thou, Marcellus shalt be!   Bring lilies, full hand-
    fuls of lilies,
Let me strew blossoms of purple; at least, let me
    offer thy spirit

These little tokens of love, and render this trivial
    tribute!"   885
   So, throughout all that bright country, they wan-
    dered on hither and thither
Over wide, airy plains, and noted each mountain
    and valley.
After Anchises hath guided his son through the
    vistas of Heaven,
When he hath kindled his soul with desire for a
    glorious future,
Then of the wars that are soon to be waged he
    speaks to the hero;   890
Tells of Laurentian tribes, and tells of the town
    of Latinus;
Teaching both how to avoid and how to endure
    each misfortune.
   Twain are the gates of Sleep, and of these, by
    common tradition,
One is of horn, whereby true visions pass easily
    upward;
Fashioned of ivory fair, the other is white and
    resplendent,   895
Yet are the dreams untrue that the Spirits release
    through its portals.
Here, having spoken these words to his son and
    the Sibyl, Anchises
Halted his steps, and then, through the ivory gate-
    way dismissed them.
He by the speediest way returns to his ships and
    his comrades.
Coasting the shore to the right he comes to the
    port of Cajeta;   900
Anchor from prow is dropped, and the sterns are
    at rest on the seashore.

𝕮𝖍𝖊 𝕽𝖎𝖇𝖊𝖗𝖘𝖎𝖉𝖊 𝕻𝖗𝖊𝖘𝖘

Electrotyped and printed by H. O Houghton & Co.
Cambridge, Mass , U S. A

CPSIA information can be obtained
at www.ICGtesting.com
Printed in the USA
BVHW041010140119
537773BV00014B/1046/P